A GREATER PURPOSE

Finding Your Place in God's Great Big Space

Mark Hughes

Dedication

To my loving family, who provided me with a lifetime of sermon and book illustrations and never once complained that I was airing our dirty laundry—even though I clearly was.

And to Church of the Rock, my faith family, who gave me the opportunity to learn to share God's Word and then, most amazingly, responded by putting it into practice in their own lives in a way that I could only have dreamed.

Contents

Introduction

To exist in this vast universe for a speck of time is the great gift of life. Our tiny sliver of time is our gift of life. It is our only life. The universe will go on, indifferent to our brief existence, but while we are here we touch not just part of that vastness, but also the lives around us.

— Terry Goodkind[1]

IN THE 1970s, the trend among young people was to spend at least a few months travelling through Europe before resuming "normal" life in North America. There was a slew of books written on how to do Europe "on the cheap," like *Europe on $5 a Day*. The quirkiest of all these how-to books was *The Hitchhiker's Guide to Europe*. For example, it emphatically stated that there was really only one essential must-have item, and that was a towel. If you had your own towel, you had it made.

My older brother Brad was one of those young people who headed off to Europe to discover the world and grow his hair long. When he left, he was wearing his hair like Paul McCartney did in his early days, but when he returned, he looked more like Ozzy Osbourne. He was also sporting the requisite pierced ear that he had inflicted upon himself with a sewing needle. Apparently it hurt a lot more than he had expected. The older generation was not yet comfortable with the long hair thing, so my father tried to shame him into a haircut by calling him "Brenda." It didn't work. Brad followed

1

The Hitchhiker's Guide to Europe religiously and survived six months with only a few hundred dollars and one towel. When he returned home to Canada, my mother didn't wash the towel—she had to burn it. *The Hitchhiker's Guide to Europe* was, and still is, the number one book stolen from libraries.

During this same period, Douglas Adams from England was trekking through Europe following the not so timeless principles of the "Guide," and wondered why no one had written a guide for "hitch-hiking around the galaxy."[2] That inspiration led to him write the bizarre story, *The Hitchhikers Guide to the Galaxy*. It became a hit radio show on the BBC, and eventually Adams wrote five books based on the radio series. He has a huge cult following even today and the five books have sold over 15 million copies. In 2005, it was made into a big screen movie. If you are under thirty-five, you have probably seen it. If you are over thirty-five, you probably don't want to. It is an utterly inane, bizarre, yet entirely entertaining story. Adam's journey across the cosmos was all in jest, but his motivation was not. Who doesn't need a hitchhikers guide to the galaxy? We all feel insignificant in the great expanse of the universe.

When you begin to consider that you came into this world as only a single sperm, competing against 250 million others for the right to fertilize your mother's egg, only to discover that you were only one of 7 billion other people trying to find our place on planet Earth, which turned out to be only one of nine other planets (if you count Pluto—it will always be a planet in my books) in a solar system that is only one of 200 million others in a galaxy (the Milky Way), which is only one of 200 million other galaxies in a universe that is 13.67 billion light years across . . . it is perhaps only human to feel a little lost in space. Our universe is so far beyond our comprehension that we cannot even begin to understand it. The only reasonable conclusion is that we are nothing more than a speck in time. Yet God, the Creator of all of this, says,

> *"Blessed be the God and Father of our Lord Jesus Christ, who has blessed us with every spiritual blessing in the heavenly places in Christ, just as He chose us in Him before the foundation of the world . . ."*
>
> EPHESIANS 1:3–4

God chose each and every one of us before He created any of this. Not one single person is an accident or a freak of nature. We all emerged, not from the primordial ooze but from the heart of God, with a divine purpose for being here. Therefore, no one is insignificant. No one's life is without meaning and destiny. We may be a mere speck in a vast universe, but because of Him who created each of us, we can all find our place in God's great big space.

If you have never read *A Hitchhikers Guide to the Galaxy*,[3] I'll save you the trouble of buying the book and get right to the point. The story revolves around building a supercomputer called Deep Thought, and after it runs a program for 7½ million years it spits out the answer to life, the universe, and everything.

The answer is 42.

If you have seen the movie, you will think that's funny. Again, if you haven't seen it, it will just sound plain stupid. Both conclusions are correct. The computer goes on to suggest that what we really need to know is The Ultimate Question! The computer says, "So once you do know what the question actually is, you'll know what the answer means."[4]

As convoluted as that sounds, there is an important premise here. The first step in answering any question is to know the right question. The answer 42 makes perfect sense if the question is 6 x 7 but not much sense if the question at hand is the meaning of life, the universe and everything. THAT is the correct question. Everyone wants answers to life, the universe and everything. Everyone!

Author Stephen Hawking wrote books about space, time, astrophysics and black holes, but they were really scientific attempts to answer the question of the meaning of life. I would go as far as to say that Hawking was desperate to know that answer. He even called one of his theories the theory of everything. At the end of *A Brief History of Time*, Hawking drew this conclusion:

> However, if we do discover a complete theory, it should in time be understandable in broad principle by everyone, not just a few scientists. Then we shall all, philosophers, scientists, and just ordinary people, be able to take part in the discussion of the question of why it is that we and the universe exist. If we find the answer to that, it would be the ultimate triumph of human reason—for then we would know the mind of God.[5]

Hawking seemed to be suggesting that the existence of God was necessary to explain the origin of the universe. The book went on to be a bestseller with over 9 million copies sold, making the Oxford cosmologist a household name in many circles. Hawking later admitted that he almost omitted this concluding line from his book and believed that had he done so sales would have been less than half. Why? Because the world is anxious to know the meaning of life, the universe and everything. Once you take God out of the equation, you are not even close to an answer. Which, sadly, is exactly what Hawking did in later musings.

> We are each free to believe what we want and it is my view that the simplest explanation is there is no God. No one created the universe and no one directs our fate. This leads me to a profound realization. There is probably no heaven,

and no afterlife either. We have this one life to appreciate the grand design of the universe, and for that, I am extremely grateful.[6]

IF JESUS IS THE ANSWER, THEN WHAT IS THE QUESTION?

No answer makes sense if we don't know the question. This whole concept of understanding the big question first dawned on me one day as I was driving my mini-van behind a modern day Wiccan. Her assortment of bumper stickers gave her away: "My other car is a broom," "Tastes like Wiccan" (whatever that means—tastes like chicken?) and, "If Jesus is the answer, then what is the question?" That was the one that got me thinking. Jesus makes no sense if people don't know what the question is.

If people do not know that they are fallen sinners in need of salvation, then Jesus has little significance to them. That is a crucial question indeed, and it's the subject of countless books. But is it the big question? Perhaps, but I think there is an even bigger question.

If Stephen Hawking has overcomplicated the question, we preachers have oversimplified it: "You are a sinner going to hell. You need Jesus. The end." We need to at least try to back up the train a bit and look at the big picture. There has to be a reason for us to be here in the first place. It all makes no sense unless every single one of us has a God-given destiny and purpose. I can't believe for a minute that the whole thing was a biological accident and that we just crawled out of the primordial ooze to live for a season and return to the ground as worm food. If that is all there is to it, then Paul the apostle was correct when he said, *"If the dead do not rise, 'Let us eat and drink, for tomorrow we die!'"* (1 Corinthians 15:32). Existence itself becomes meaningless. Morality is really not that important if human life has no intrinsic value. Which, incidentally, is exactly why societies fall into abject moral decay when they abandon their belief in a Creator.

The bigger question has to be Why do we exist in the first place? Why did He create the earth? The heavens? The universe? This question is so big that all others hang upon it. Why did He stick each of us in the midst of it? Why did God create us? For what *greater purpose* does each of us exist? It is a question that we all ask, in one form or another, sinner and saint alike. If we can answer that question, we can better understand our own destiny. If we can't, we will never understand life.

The greatest thinkers of all time have wrestled with the big question of existence. The seventeenth-century French philosopher Rene Descartes gave the simplest answer: « *Je pense, donc je suis,* » which translates to, "I think, therefore I am." Hmm . . . excuse me while I think about that. The joke goes like this: Descartes goes into a bar. The bartender asks, "Rene would you like one for the road?" Descartes says, "I think not—" and POOF he disappears!

This book is about answering the big question. It is not another book about self-actualization and maximizing your human potential. There have been enough books written about "becoming all you can be" and setting new sales records or being employee of the month for the twelfth time this year. It is about discovering your *greater purpose* in life. It is about finding meaning in a world that is often confusing and misleading. It is about *finding your place in God's great big space.* As Terry Goodkind quipped, it is about "not only touching the vastness of the universe but the lives of those around us."[7] Ah, there's the rub. Our destiny is ultimately wrapped up in the lives of those around us.

As a pastor, I do a lot of funerals. I see people at the very end of their journey, and I can say with extreme certainty that the only real difference we make in this life is how we impact the lives of those around us while we are here.

There is one biblical text that I will refer to again and again throughout the pages of this book, and that is Philippians 3:13–14.

> *Brethren, I do not count myself to have apprehended; but one thing I do, forgetting those things which are behind and reaching forward to those things which are ahead, I press toward the goal for the prize of the upward call of God in Christ Jesus.*

Paul says here that, for all his pursuits in life, his greatest is to *"lay hold of that for which Christ Jesus has also laid hold of me"* (Philippians 3:12). In other words, he continually strives to lay hold of God's purpose for his life. There is no higher aspiration than this. Even the great apostle Paul, who wrote two-thirds of the New Testament and "turned his world upside down" (Acts 17:6), still wrestled to try and find his destiny in God. If he, of all people, felt as if he had not yet arrived, is it not any wonder the rest of us do as well?

WHAT REALLY MATTERS IS NOT WHAT WE ACTUALLY
ACCOMPLISH BUT THAT WE COMMIT OUR LIVES TO
PURSUING GOD'S PURPOSES.

Perhaps the most important thing I will say in this entire book is this: what really matters is not what we actually accomplish but that we commit our lives to pursuing God's purposes. Whether we feel like we changed our world, or not, is not nearly as important as the sense of fulfillment that we at least attempted to lay hold of that for which Christ Jesus laid hold of us. I am thoroughly convinced that it will be these people who will hear on that fateful day, *"Well done, good and faithful servant . . . Enter into the joy of your lord"* (Matthew 25:21).

You didn't choose to be born. You didn't choose to live on this planet. We all came into this world kicking and screaming—literally. You were wet, cold and bloody, and to add insult to injury, the doctor slapped you on the butt to get your attention and then, in a Darth Vader-like voice said, "Welcome to planet Earth. Enjoy your stay." There was nothing you could do about it except cry unless, of course you were born Chuck Norris. When he was born, the doctor slapped him on the backside. Fortunately for the doctor, he was already in a hospital.

The Bible refers to us as sojourners or "strangers in the land" (Hebrews 11:13, 1 Peter 2:11). We are all going along for the ride, and none of us are in the driver's seat, so we had better figure out why we are here.

Years ago, famous cosmologist Carl Sagan insisted that the universe has other life forms on other planets, perhaps even entire alien civilizations. Movies like *Star Trek*, *Star Wars* and *Avatar* have only served to reinforce the belief that we are not alone in the universe. The idea appeals to our human nature because there is something eerie about the thought that we might be on the only inhabited planet, floating aimlessly like a speck in a universe that is some 13 billion light years across. It really doesn't matter what worldview one comes from, we all long to see the bigger picture.

Today, science is clearly beginning to challenge Sagan's speculations. Modern astronomers have noted that there are certain characteristics about our universe—and planet Earth in particular (like the ratio of the gravitational force constant to the electromagnetic force constant)—that are so specific that if they were altered, even slightly, our planet could not contain human life. Today, 153 finely tuned characteristics have been identified.[8] If there was any slight change in the way the universe exists, it could not sustain human life.

The chance of there being life in the universe at all is one trillionth of one trillionth percent.[9] That means the odds that any given planet in the universe would possess the necessary conditions to support intelligent physical life is a number so large it might as well be infinity. We are breaking all the odds. There are some 100 billion solar systems like ours in our galaxy, the Milky Way, and there are 100 billion galaxies in the universe—are we so certain our planet is the only one that can sustain life?

Science is now strongly suggesting that we are not a fluke of nature and that the entire universe was designed so mankind could have a place to live. This has become known as the Anthropic Principle, which upholds that the universe appears to be "designed" for the sake of human life.

> *This is the history of the heavens and the earth when they were created, in the day that the Lord God made the earth and the heavens, before any plant of the field was in the earth and before any herb of the field had grown. For the Lord God had not caused it to rain on the earth, and there was no man to till the ground; but a mist went up from the earth and watered the whole face of the ground. And the Lord God formed man of the dust of the ground, and breathed into his nostrils the breath of life; and man became a living being. The Lord God planted a garden eastward in Eden, and there He put the man whom He had formed.*
>
> GENESIS 2:4–8

The bottom line is this: the universe exists for the purpose of sustaining human life. God created the heavens and earth and stars. He made the universe stretch out, all 13.67 billion light years of it, and put us right in the midst of it. It is mind boggling beyond comprehension. None of our finite, peanut-sized brains are capable of understanding a universe of these dimensions. No one is able to comprehend a Creator who could have framed it all together as marvellously as He did with such excruciating attention to the minutest detail. And the more we learn about God's creation, the more in awe we should become.

During the time of Alexander the Great, the conqueror of the mighty Grecian empire, an indigent philosopher of Alexander's court sought relief at his hand. The philosopher was given the authority to receive from Alexander's treasurer any sum he should ask. He immediately demanded ten thousand pounds. The treasurer balked at the extravagant amount, but Alexander replied, "Let the money be instantly paid. I am delighted with this philosopher's way of thinking. He has done me a singular honour. By the largeness of his request, he shows the high idea he has conceived of my wealth and munificence."[10]

The extravagance of the universe is, of course, a reflection of God, not of us. The Scripture says that when we look upon it, creation itself declares the Creator. It is the height of human arrogance to think that any of it could exist without Him.

> *For since the creation of the world His invisible attributes are clearly seen, being understood by the things that are made, even His eternal power and Godhead, so that they are without excuse, because, although they knew God, they did not glorify Him as God, nor were thankful, but became futile in their thoughts, and their foolish hearts were darkened. Professing to be wise, they became fools, and changed the glory of the incorruptible God into an image made like corruptible man—and birds and four-footed animals and creeping things.*
>
> ROMANS 1:20–23

In 2003, after thirteen years of mapping the entire human DNA, the Human Genome Project was completed. They identified 20,500 human genes consisting of 3.3 million chemical base pairs in every human cell. Other than identical twins, all 7 billion people on the planet have a combination unique to them. After the project was completed, the lead scientist, Dr. Francis Collins, sat down and wrote a book called *The Language of God: A Scientist Presents Evidence for Belief.*[11] He was overwhelmed by God's creation and needed to express it in an unashamed way to the world. Imagine the stir he caused among his colleagues. The scientific community has not always been comfortable with such open declarations of faith.

Collins' story is an interesting one. In the 1970s, as a medical student, he was an avowed atheist. He saw no reason or need for the existence of God. After he graduated and started practicing medicine, however, his life was not so academic. He began to encounter the life and death issues of his patients. In the face of terminal diagnoses they asked, "What do you believe, doctor?" The science he loved so much was powerless to answer the really important questions.

> *If the universe had a beginning, then who created it?*
> *Why are the physical constants in the universe so finely tuned*
> *   to allow the possibility of complex life forms?*
> *Why do humans have a moral sense?*
> *What happens after we die?*
> *What is the meaning of life?*
> *Why are we here?*
> *Why does mathematics work, anyway?*

Slowly but surely, as Collins turned to the Scriptures and the Christian faith, the answers to life's most challenging questions began to emerge (although the math one is not as clearly addressed). The Human Genome Project only served to cement his sentiment that creation was not—and could not be— a fluke of nature but rather a divine act of a sovereign God. Collins puts it this way.

> Will we turn our backs on science because it is perceived as a threat to God, abandoning all the promise of advancing our understanding of nature and applying that to the alleviation of suffering and the betterment of humankind? Alternatively, will we turn our backs on faith, concluding that science has rendered the spiritual life no longer necessary, and that traditional religious symbols can now be replaced by engravings of the double helix on our alters? Both of these choices are profoundly dangerous. Both deny truth. Both will diminish the nobility of humankind. Both will be devastating to our future. And both are unnecessary. The God of the Bible is also the God of the genome. He can be worshipped in the cathedral or in the laboratory. His creation is majestic, awesome, intricate and beautiful—and it cannot be at war with itself. Only we imperfect humans can start such battles. And only we can end them.
>
> . . . If humans evolved strictly by mutation and natural selection, who needs God to explain us? To this, I reply: I do. The comparison of chimp and human sequences, interesting as it is, does not tell us what it means to be human. In my views, DNA sequence alone, even if accompanied by a vast trove of data on biological function, will never explain certain special human attributes, such as the knowledge of the Moral Law and the universal search for God. Freeing God from the burden of special acts of creation does not remove Him as the source of the things that make humanity special, and of the universe itself. It merely shows us something of how He operates.[12]

In a way, this is the same place that a much humbler King David arrived while he was still a shepherd boy lying out in the fields at night.

When I consider Your heavens, the work of Your fingers,
The moon and the stars, which You have ordained,
What is man that You are mindful of him,
And the son of man that You visit him?

PSALM 8:3–4

He, too, was asking the big questions, and he, too, was just trying to find his place in God's great big space.

Chapter One

Cookies and Other Distractions

"COOKIES!!! UMM-NUM-NUM-NUM-NUM!!!"

— Cookie Monster

IN THE LATE 1960s, Stanford University psychology professor Walter Mischel developed what he called the Marshmallow Test.[1] He claimed he could predict the future success of four-year-olds based on how they handled his Marshmallow Test. He would place them alone in a room with a single marshmallow. He told them if they wanted, they could just ring a little bell and eat the marshmallow at any time. However, if they waited for him to return from an errand, he would bring with him a second marshmallow and then they would have two to eat. One-third of the four-year-olds ate it immediately, one-third ate sometime within the twenty minutes, and one-third waited the full twenty minutes and received a second marshmallow.

Before you read any further, ask yourself what you would have done as a four-year-old. Most people can remember exactly what kind of kid they were. I'll tell you a little later how I think I would have done. I actually know.

The really fascinating part of the experiment was that Mischel continued to track his test subjects into adulthood. He discovered that those who waited to eat the marshmallow became far more successful as adults. They did better in school, were more likely to go to college, had better relationships and careers, and scored a remarkable 210 points higher on their Scholastic Aptitude Tests. The most impulsive of the group, who ate immediately, were most likely to be bullies or have behavioural problems in school. They were also more prone to get involved with drugs, less likely to go to college, and struggled in their careers and relationships. The results were so consistent that Mischel became confident he could predict any child's future level of success with a single marshmallow.

I wrote a blog on this subject and some readers were understandably offended to think a marshmallow can determine a child's fate. Rest assured that I do not believe anyone is doomed to failure because they ate a marshmallow. On the contrary, in Christ every one of us is destined for greatness. Nevertheless, I feel Mischel's findings are helpful in understanding human weaknesses. Impulsive children grow up to be impulsive adults. They are always looking for instant gratification. Studies show that this generation will have an average of seven different careers. Not seven different jobs, but seven completely different careers! There is nothing wrong with a little variety.

I did many things myself before I entered the ministry. I worked in retail and construction, ran the family farm, started training to be a pilot, and even tried my hand at sales. Variety is the spice of life, after all, but here's the problem: if you have seven different careers, then that means you are starting over seven different times. You almost always start anything at the bottom, not the top.

People who start over too often never get good at anything. The generation before us would pick a career path and stick to it for their entire lives. By the end of their run they were very skillful, very well paid, and usually able to live off the fruits of their former labours. On the other hand, I have friends who are fifty-five years old and still trying to "find themselves" and settle into a career path. They have little savings, little (if any) pension, and they will have to keep slogging along for many years to come.

The scenario does not stop with vocation. We see the same trend with modern families. Couples are still getting divorced at unprecedented rates and finding new mates with whom to "start over." I have one friend my age who now has children and grandchildren who are the same age as each other. That's not really normal unless you are some sort of tribal king with twelve wives who is constantly adding a new virgin to the harem. The marshmallow syndrome follows us for our entire lives, influencing everything we do as we continually look for the next quick fix or sure thing.

One of the running gags on TV's *The Simpsons* is Homer's weakness for donuts. Many people fail to see the brilliance in the *Simpsons* cartoon. If you just watch the episodes without thinking about them, you are really missing something. I am constantly surprised by how many Christian people in particular find the cartoon offensive. Many fail to see the intended social commentary on everything that is wrong with modern North American culture. The writers have a knack for skewering many of us through the idiosyncrasies of Homer and Bart, the classic underachievers. The donut gag is basically an adult version of the Marshmallow Test. In a Halloween episode, Homer's head was turned into a giant donut. This was problematic for Homer because he could not stop eating it.

> Marge: "Homer, stop eating your head."
> Homer: "But I'm so yummy . . ."[2]

In another episode, Homer sold his soul to the Devil for a single donut.[3] The Devil, by the way, appeared to him at the home of Ned Flanders, Homer's goody-two-shoes Christian neighbour. That alone was an immensely clever touch, since the temptations of the Devil rarely appear as terrifying and grotesque but as safe and appealing. In

Genesis 3:1–5 we discover that the Devil said to Eve, *"You shall not die, but God knows that if you eat the fruit you will be like Him knowing both good and evil"* (vv. 4–5). The temptation seemed like a good thing coming from an appealing character. In fact, the story alerts us at the outset that *"the Serpent was more cunning than any beast of the field"* (Genesis 3:1).

When I watch people who cannot control their impulses, whether it is drinking, smoking, gambling, pornography, eating, gossip or shopping, I can't help but think of the Marshmallow Test. Billions fail the test every day and then can't figure out why life isn't more satisfying. They buy the new shoes, car, iPod, computer or whatever, and the next day they feel as empty as they did the day before.

As much as many people get the impression from my speaking that I invented ADHD, I actually have a huge amount of self-discipline. We did the Marshmallow Test every week in our house as I was growing up. Our family stockpiled huge bags of puffed wheat the size of Prince Edward Island in order to feed the hungry mob called my siblings. Every once in a while my mother would buy a single box of Alpha-Bits cereal. This was a special treat, roughly equivalent to a family Disney vacation today. My mother would say, "Okay, here is the deal; everybody gets one bowl each."

When the box arrived home from the grocery store, it never made it to the pantry. The bowls and the milk would come out and the feeding frenzy would begin. Naively, I always said, "Make sure you leave a bowl for me. I am saving mine for breakfast tomorrow." The next morning I would find the box, all right . . . with nothing more than some powdery sugar at the bottom. One Sunday I told this story to my congregation and added the comment in jest, "And to this day I have never tasted Alpha-Bits." That next week I had maybe five boxes of Alpha-Bits arrive at my office. Turns out, I don't even really like Alpha-Bits!

If you were to look at the Alpha-Bits story in isolation, it might seem like I was pretty much a loser. I lost out again and again, right? Wrong! Instant gratification is the most empty of all things. Once the marshmallow is gone, it is gone. Nobody sits around reliving the memory of a cookie or donut. *I remember the summer of '87, I had a Crispy Cream donut like no other. That moment may carry me for the rest of my life.* No, it's gone and forgotten. The more enduring question becomes, how has the Marshmallow Test (in my case, Alpha-Bits) affected my adulthood? I really haven't changed. I had a box of chocolates that I got for Christmas one year that I didn't open until the next Christmas, when I received yet another box from the same person. I've discovered I have Herculean will power. I can outwait or outlast any opponent.

This kind of semi-insanity has proved to be invaluable in ministry. The fruit or results of ministry come painfully slow. Sometimes you don't see any evidence of your labour for years. But God rewards faithfulness . . . always.

> *His lord said to him, "Well done, good and faithful servant; you have been faithful over a few things, I will make you ruler over many things. Enter into the joy of your lord."*
>
> MATTHEW 25:23

There is another aspect to this that I don't want you to miss. If you ask someone what they really want out of life, they will almost always give you the same answer: HAPPINESS. And how do you make someone happy? Give them a cookie! COOKIES make us HAPPY.

One year on our cross-Canada tour, I asked the question, "How many of you would be happy if I gave you a cookie?" Many in the audiences responded favourably. Then I pulled out a box of cookies and started throwing them into the crowd. People would catch them and start munching gleefully. Then I addressed those eating the cookies, asking "Are you happy?" Smiling, they would nod up and down, unable to talk since their mouths were jammed full of cookies. Then I cruelly mocked them and told them that I had just reduced them to the level of four-year-olds. That's how you make a four-year-old happy. Give him a cookie. The audience members never cared; they just sat smiling and munching.

JOY IS VERY DIFFERENT THAN HAPPINESS BECAUSE IT HAS NOTHING TO DO WITH CIRCUMSTANCES.

The whole point of that exercise was to demonstrate how happiness is externally prompted. If something good happens, we are happy. If something bad happens, we are sad. If you get a raise at work, you are happy. If you lose your job, you are sad. If you get a new car, you are happy. When you get your first parking lot ding in it, you are sad. If you get married, you are happy. If you get divorced . . . hmmm, I better not go there. The problem with happiness is that it is almost entirely based on externals. Those who seek "happiness" live on a constant roller coaster of emotions determined entirely by the circumstances of life.

There is an alternative.

Joy is very different than happiness because it has nothing to do with circumstances. What the Bible really promises us is joy, not happiness. Joy is mentioned 150 times in the Bible, mostly in the context of God giving it to us.

You will show me the path of life;
In Your presence is fullness of joy;
At Your right hand are pleasures forevermore.

PSALM 16:11

One of the remarkable aspects of true joy is that you can have it even in the midst of terrible circumstances. Your world can be falling apart at the seams, but you can still find joy in the middle of it all. The apostle James put it this way,

> *My brethren, count it all joy when you fall into various trials, knowing that the testing of your faith produces patience. But let patience have its perfect work, that you may be perfect and complete, lacking nothing.*
>
> JAMES 1:2–4

Count it all joy? Okay, he was either both completely and utterly insane or he knew something we don't know. I think it was the latter. James knew that not only is joy not predicated on the circumstances, it is also the key to overcoming the circumstances. It would seem that joy is somehow a catalyst for allowing our faith to work in the face of adversity. It is really hard to embrace our failures and setbacks as good things. We encounter some sort of setback almost every day. The challenge is to find a way to turn the stumbling block into a stepping-stone.

In 1942, an Austrian Jew by the name of Victor Frankl was arrested, along with his wife and parents, and taken to a German concentration camp. Even though Frankl was a trained physician in both neurology and psychiatry, he was treated no better than any other captive. During this time of unspeakable injustice, he watched helplessly as the Nazis murdered his wife and parents. Frankl managed to survive the war and eventually returned to his profession as a psychiatrist.

After the war he wrote thirty-two books, the most famous being *Man's Search for Meaning.* Frankl recalls the lowest point of his time in the German concentration camp. He was standing along with the other male prisoners, naked, starving and humiliated. A guard noticed his gold wedding ring on his finger and casually walked over and cut it off. In that moment this thought came to him: *You can take my wife and my parents, strip me of my clothes and my freedom. But there is one thing you cannot take away from me: my freedom to choose how I will react to what happens to me.*[4] In other words, irrespective of what the external circumstances looked like, he realized he always had the power to choose his response. Frankl's hallmark conclusion was that, even in the most absurd, painful and dehumanized situation, life has potential meaning, and therefore, even suffering is meaningful. Here is an excerpt from *Man's Search for Meaning* regarding his time working in the harsh conditions of the Auschwitz concentration camp:

> We stumbled on in the darkness, over big stones and through large puddles, along the one road leading from the camp. The accompanying guards kept shouting at us and driving us with the butts of their rifles. Anyone with very sore feet supported himself on his neighbor's arm. Hardly a word was spoken; the icy wind did not encourage talk. Hiding his mouth behind his upturned collar, the man marching next to me whispered suddenly: "If our wives could see us now! I do hope they are better off in their camps and don't know what is happening to us."
>
> That brought thoughts of my own wife to mind. And as we stumbled on for miles, slipping on icy spots, supporting each other time and again, dragging one another up and onward, nothing was said, but we both knew: each of us was thinking of his wife. Occasionally I looked at the sky, where the stars were fading and the pink light of the morning was beginning to spread behind a dark bank of clouds. But my mind clung to my wife's image, imagining it with an uncanny acuteness. I heard her answering me, saw her smile, her frank and encouraging

look. Real or not, her look was then more luminous than the sun which was beginning to rise.

A thought transfixed me: for the first time in my life I saw the truth as it is set into song by so many poets, proclaimed as the final wisdom by so many thinkers. The truth—that love is the ultimate and the highest goal to which man can aspire. Then I grasped the meaning of the greatest secret that human poetry and human thought and belief have to impart: The salvation of man is through love and in love. I understood how a man who has nothing left in this world still may know bliss, be it only for a brief moment, in the contemplation of his beloved. In a position of utter desolation, when man cannot express himself in positive action, when his only achievement may consist in enduring his sufferings in the right way—an honorable way—in such a position man can, through loving contemplation of the image he carries of his beloved, achieve fulfillment. For the first time in my life I was able to understand the meaning of the words, "The angels are lost in perpetual contemplation of an infinite glory..."[5]

Frankl suffered more than I hope any of us will ever have to know, yet in the midst of it he was able to find "bliss." He put forward the simple concept that everyone has the power to choose their response, and consequently their attitude, regardless of the situation they are facing. Unfortunately, people do not believe that today. They ride the emotional roller coaster up and down and complain bitterly when things don't go their way. Life is so wonderful and teeming full of God's beauty, God's people, and God's purpose, yet too many of us look for momentary happiness in temporal and ephemeral things.

JOY COMES FROM WITHIN

Happiness may come from external things like cookies and donuts, but joy comes from within.

> *In this you greatly rejoice, though now for a little while, if need be, you have been grieved by various trials, that the genuineness of your faith, being much more precious than gold that perishes, though it is tested by fire, may be found to praise, honor, and glory at the revelation of Jesus Christ, whom having not seen you love. Though now you do not see Him, yet believing, you rejoice with joy inexpressible and full of glory.*
>
> 1 PETER 1:6–8

The apostle Peter was writing to Christians who were suffering intense persecution, and yet he tells them to "*greatly rejoice.*" Uh huh! He goes on to explain that because of their relationship with Jesus Christ they had "*joy inexpressible.*" Whatever that was, it clearly had nothing to do with the circumstances around them, which were nothing short of abysmal. They were losing their jobs, their freedom and their lives. They had to look within to find joy, and ultimately, the greater purpose for their lives. I suppose there is nothing easy about this, but I know it is possible.

LIFE IS SO WONDERFUL AND TEEMING FULL OF GOD'S BEAUTY, GOD'S PEOPLE, AND GOD'S PURPOSE, YET TOO MANY OF US LOOK FOR MOMENTARY HAPPINESS IN TEMPORAL AND EPHEMERAL THINGS.

Karen is a single mom and a career waitress, whom we met thirty years ago, before we even had children. We go to her restaurant for lunch on my day off and she is almost always our server. She has an easy and effervescent personality and we fell in love with her early on. One week we invited her and her then-husband to church. They had never really been to a church like ours and the experience was overwhelming. During the singing she became so uncomfortable that she ran out of the building. I knew the music was bad but I didn't think it was that bad! Later we went for lunch, and the feelings she described as we visited sounded a lot like the work of the Holy Spirit plowing deep into her heart. We decided to pull back and let God work on her after that, which He did. Within a year she came to Christ and started attending a different church. She still thought we were kind of whacko. After a couple of years, she showed up again at our church and has been there for many years now.

Karen has been good with her money and has managed to buy a house and raise a beautiful daughter. Nevertheless, she needs to live very carefully to make ends meet. One Sunday I was preaching on being an overcomer. She left the service flying high and ready to take on another week.

When she got into the parking lot, she discovered that her car had a flat tire. Not only that, she had committed the cardinal sin of driving on it flat and the tire was toast. She called a tow truck, and by the time she had a new tire on the car, she was out over $200. She tried to convince herself that she was still an overcomer and that she would find a way to make it up that week.

The next day at work someone at the restaurant did a "dine and dash" and left without paying their bill. Her boss held the waitresses responsible when that happened and Karen had to pay for the $57 lunch bill. She broke down at work and wept. At this point she no longer felt like an overcomer and decided she was going to call me up and give me a piece of her mind that "this overcomer attitude stuff isn't working!" She was half joking and we had a laugh about it and prayed together that God would come to her rescue.

The next Sunday I was still preaching about overcoming and shared her story because people needed to know that things don't always work out in the short-term. We are still overcomers even if it doesn't look like it or feel like it. Jesus said, *"In the world you will have tribulation; but be of good cheer, I have overcome the world"* (John 16:33).

After the service was over, a man I had never seen before came up to me and asked if I could do him a favour. He pulled $257 cash out of his wallet and said, "Give this to that waitress. She needs to know that God is always faithful." He turned and walked away and I never saw him again. I did the only reasonable thing and pocketed the cash! No . . . I found Karen and gave her the money. She started to cry and gave me a big hug. I have discovered that women only cry at two times—when they are sad and when they are happy.

This is a great outcome, but I need to be clear that not every story has a happy ending. Sometimes, like the bumper sticker says, "Stuff happens!" It is "stuff," isn't it? We look at the circumstance and it is impossible to see how anything good came out of it. Sometimes we cannot see the greater purpose in a situation. We just have to accept by faith that God is still on the throne and somehow, some way, He is doing something.

> *"And we know that <u>all things</u> work together for good to those who love God, to those who are the called according to His purpose."*
>
> ROMANS 8:28, *emphasis added*

This verse does not say all *good* things work together; it says *all things* work together for *good*. There is a big difference. It tells us that if we will love God, keep a right attitude and look for God's purpose in everything, He will cause it to work together for good.

While I was writing this chapter, my resolve got tested on this very point. I had blocked off a certain amount of time to get it finished and was avoiding distractions and therefore anything that would prevent me from making my deadline. After a very good morning of writing, I decided to take a short break and do a small household project that had been put off too long. There was a little metal molding on the bottom of the oven door that had started to rust. The stove, though fairly old, still looked great. It had three small screws holding the molding on. I planned to pop them off, sand the surface, hit it with spray paint and get back to writing. Fifteen to twenty minutes, tops.

As I removed the last screw, the front panel of the oven door (which was glass) literally exploded on top of me. I had not realized that the molding held the glass in place. Once it came loose from its frame, it shattered before it even hit the ground. It was as if a glass hand grenade had gone off. I lay on the floor covered in fragments of safety glass. I was unharmed but in a mild state of shock.

The better part of the next hour was spent cleaning up glass that was somehow in almost every room of the house. Then I started phoning around, trying to find the part, only to discover that it would be almost as expensive as replacing the stove. I decided I would just buy a good used one, since it needed to match the other appliances and a new one would not. I loaded the old stove in the van and drove forty-five minutes to a place that had an entire room of used stoves.

As I walked in the door, I discovered that they had a stove that was an exact match. I could not believe my good fortune. Surely God had smiled on me and I was going to get back to writing in no time. It turned out the owner of this back lane establishment was a Christian and he was thrilled to help a pastor solve his problem. He took the old one off my hands and a couple hours later I had the new one installed, hooked up and ready to go . . . only to discover that the digital screen on the stove did not work. The thing was shot. I was right back where I had started.

The next day I called the cheery proprietor and we decided that the simplest fix would be to swap the digital screen with the panel from my old stove, which I knew worked, and it would be good to go. I had looked at it and it was only two screws and three snap-on connectors. Ten minutes, tops. Once again, I went across town and two hours later was back home with the module. As I removed the broken one, to my absolute shock, I discovered that the connectors were completely different and it was not going to work without rewiring the whole thing. I was not going to do that.

Once again I called my new best friend, who told me just to bring it all back and get another. At this point it was very hard to keep a good attitude. I was not very happy in the first place that this guy had promised me a working stove, when in reality he had never tested it. Carrying stoves in and out of the house up the stairs was getting to be less joyful each time. Nevertheless, I was determined it was all good and there was going to be some big happy ending that would, at the very least, make a great sermon illustration.

This time when I went back to the store, I made sure the stove was plugged in and I tested every feature. Two hours later I was hauling another stove up the steps. As I went to plug it in, I discovered that it had a four-prong plug and I had a three-prong receptacle. I wanted to cry, but instead I broke out in laughter. Kathy wanted to know what was so funny. I told her about the plug, laughing hysterically as I explained to her why it was not going to work.

She said, "Are you alright?"

"No, how could I be?" I stated, adding to her confusion, "That's what is so funny."

To make a long, boring story even longer, I replaced the plug and cord with a three-pronged one and eventually had the stove back running again.

Two days of my life were gone and I was right back where I had started before I had touched the oven door. It was two days I would never get back. It was time I had lost out of my writing schedule and there was nothing I could do about it. If this book seems shorter than you think it should be, that is why. Stuff happens!

More importantly, I managed not to lose my joy. Joy comes from within and has nothing to do with what happens on the outside. The key to maintaining that joy is to always remember that, whether we see it or not, God is always at work and that *all things work together for good to those who love God, to those who are the called according to His purpose* (Romans 8:28).

Chapter Two

Male Mental Pause
and Other Detours

*If someone has a mid-life crisis while playing hide and seek,
does he automatically lose because he can't find himself?*

— Unknown

EVERY ADULT MALE (and female) is familiar with the modern
phenomenon we call the *mid-life crisis.* I prefer to call it *male mental
pause.* The otherwise sane middle-aged man suddenly starts to do
strange and bizarre things. He buys a sports car, dons a gold chain
and wears a Speedo at the beach. It is not a pretty sight.

Women are not exempt from the mid-life crisis. Mattel's
venerable Barbie doll is now in her fifties—middle-aged for sure.
That girlish figure and bleached blonde hair . . . I don't think so.
They've come out with three all new Barbies, the first of which is Hot
Flash Barbie. You push her bellybutton and her cheeks turn red and
she starts to sweat. The Joan Rivers Barbie comes with saggy skin.
You pull the string on her back and her face tightens up like a snare
drum. (She would be happy we are still talking about her.) And
finally, Divorced Barbie, which costs a whopping $200. It sounds like
a lot of coin, but she comes complete with Ken's house, Ken's car and
Ken's boat.

Someone once described middle age as the season of life when the glass is finally half-full but you also start having to put your teeth in the glass overnight. Another definition is that it's the time of life when you realize your children and your clothes are the same age. One night my twenty-something-year-old son asked to borrow one of my suits. I agreed and commented how good the twenty-five-year-old garment looked on him. It was then that he told me he was going to a Halloween costume party. My *très chic* was his *trick or treat*.

My father was a well-respected lawyer, the quintessential family man with a wife, six children, a dog and a canary named Chirpy. Every year Chirpy would die and my parents would just replace him with another canary named Chirpy. Chirpy didn't seem to notice and neither did we. We had two station wagons. Not one but two. It took two of these gas guzzling beasts to transport the entire family to A&W to "pick the perfect size from the Burger Family."

When we went on vacation that meant we all had to cram into one of the cars. That also meant there was no room at all for luggage. Everyone had to wear all the clothes they needed for the week in multiple layers. Only the essentials could be taken along, and even they had to be strapped on the rooftop rack. There was never room for Chirpy. He was always dead when we got back.

Everyone in the neighbourhood knew when we were going on holidays because we were the only family in the neighbourhood that strapped sleeping bags in green garbage bags to the roof of the car since there was no room inside. We needed to bring the sleeping bags because, with a family of eight, no matter where we were going there would not be enough beds and at least four of us would be sleeping on the floor.

Growing up in a large family was a lot of fun, actually. If you wanted to play football or baseball, you didn't have to call up any friends, you already had a whole team. Or we could always challenge the O'Neils down the street from us to a game; they had twelve kids, all living in a three-bedroom house. They used to tell us, "The key to success in this family is to try to be the last one in at night so you can sleep on the top of the pile. Then you will be the first one up in the morning and you get the shoes." By comparison, only eight of us living in a five-bedroom house seemed like pure luxury. I have nothing but fond memories of those years.

Life changed dramatically for us when my father turned forty-five. He went through his mid-life crisis. One day he returned home with a new car—a sports car, a two-seater Mazda RX7. It should have been a tip-off, and it was. My mother said, "Who do you intend to drive around in that little car?" The obvious answer was "his girlfriend," but he failed to mention that at the time. You get the picture. He eventually divorced my mother, bought another house and married the girlfriend. The big question we all asked at the time was why? My dad seemed like he had it made; he had a successful career as a lawyer, a beautiful wife, five average kids and one genius son (it's my story and that's the way I remember it). Obviously something was missing.

Looking back at it now with the benefit of a few decades of married life experience under my belt, I think I can at least understand it. For all the good things in his life, he was never really content with what he had done with it. He always wanted to make the big score, like some of his rich clients. When I was younger, I would ask him when we were going to get a swimming pool in the back yard and he would reply, "When my ship comes in." I couldn't wait. My dad had a ship? I loved boats, and this one was a ship full of cargo that was going to make us all rich.

Well, his ship never came in. In fact, he lost almost all the money he ever made, either through bad business deals or poor stock investments. He lost $400,000 on a single business venture that was really doomed from the start. By his late forties he was already drinking heavily, and you could tell life was not at all up to what he had aspired. So, he reinvented himself. Beginning with the divorce and remarriage, he also got all new friends and even changed his religion. He went from a non-practicing Protestant to a practicing Catholic. It was really quite bizarre, since for twenty-five years the entire family attended the Catholic Church without him. When my mother, my siblings and I became Protestants, my dad, ironically, became a Catholic. He even overcame his debilitating fear of flying and started jetting around the globe. In many ways he became a different person, presumably because the old one had not lived up to his expectations. The new one didn't fare any better. He drank even more heavily, lost more money, got prostate cancer, then colon cancer, then liver cancer and then died.

Don't misunderstand me, I loved my dad dearly and respected his many good qualities deeply. That is why it was so painful to see him dismantle his life and not finish well. As I hit middle age, I was determined I was not going to repeat the same mistakes my father made. So, instead of getting a girlfriend, I fell in love with my wife all over again. Instead of the sports car, I bought a high-performance speedboat. And no, I do not wear a gold chain and I don't even own a Speedo. I'm still trying to convince Kathy that the boat is not a mid-life crisis thing—"It has room for the whole family! It's not my fault it goes so fast that no one will ride with me."

My father's story has been played out by millions of others in one way or another. On one level it is not hard to understand. At a certain point along the way, most of us will ask ourselves the question, "Is this all there is to life? I worked hard, I raised a family, put a roof over their head, braces on their teeth, food on the table. If that's all there is, that's not enough. What's in it for me?" So people try to inject a little excitement and usually succeed only in destroying everything they spent their entire lives building. There is something seriously amiss in our culture, which sends the message that unless you are a superstar—a Bill Gates, a Wayne Gretsky or a Brad Pitt—then your life has not amounted to much. That kind of sentiment never existed before mass media.

In ancient Greece, the birthplace of modern democracy, they dealt with this issue completely differently. If an individual was too popular, too rich or too famous, they considered that person a threat to the democratic balance. Annually, they had a vote and the "winner" was exiled from Athens (ostracised) for ten years until his popularity could subside. "Voting someone off the island" existed for thousands of years before *Survivor* came along. What a great system—we could get rid of Donald Trump, Kim Kardashian, Paris Hilton or anybody else we find annoying. When you think about it, we tried this with Martha Stewart, but she was only in prison for four months and came back with a vengeance. I don't know about you, but I felt a whole lot safer on the streets when Martha Stewart was behind bars.

I am starting to see some very positive signs that our culture is beginning to redefine success. Bill Gates, at one time, was the richest man in the world. He was making so much money per hour that the joke was that if he saw a $100 bill laying on the sidewalk it would not be worth his time to stop and pick it up. By forty-five years of age, he had already stepped down as CEO of Microsoft, and by fifty-three he left the day-to-day operations altogether. It was clear he no longer had the spark to carry the software giant any longer. I mean, where does a man go from being the richest man in the world? He has already made more money than it is humanly possible to spend. There was little left for him to accomplish in the technology industry except for maybe becoming the Antichrist, but there is a big line-up for that job.

So, to the surprise of the business community, Bill Gates resigned from making more money and transitioned his life into giving it away. He and his wife Melinda are full time with the Bill & Melinda Gates Foundation. So far they have donated $28 billion of their own funds to the Foundation and are hitting up their well-heeled friends for more. They have managed to get $3.5 billion out of the generally frugal Warren Buffet.[1] The Gates have publically stated that they will not be leaving their wealth to their three children, as they feel it will not be healthy for them. Gates said, "I will give the kids some money but not a meaningful percentage. Setting the number so that they need to work but they feel reasonably taken care of is hard to figure out."[2] In the meantime, the Gates are crisscrossing the planet, giving billions away to health, education and poverty related causes.

It would appear that Bill Gates is getting more fulfillment out of giving his money away than making it. Why? Because, in the words of Jesus, *"It is more blessed to give than to receive"* (Acts 20:35). There is always more fulfillment in what we do for others than what we do for ourselves. We were created that way.

In 1997, Bob Buford wrote his important first book, *Halftime: Changing Your Game Plan from Success to Significance.* Using the football analogy of how teams will often change their game plan for the second half, he was writing specifically to middle-aged folks about rethinking their life goals. He observed that most of us spend the first half of our life pursuing "success." Some of that is necessary in order to pay the bills and put the kids through college. He points out that we often have the luxury of refocusing our priorities in the second half of life since we don't have as many financial demands and there is little fulfillment in just gaining more career success and monetary gain. He thinks we need to change our game plan and begin to focus on others instead of ourselves. These are the pursuits of life that bring a sense of significance over success. Inevitably, it will revolve around helping others succeed and find their own sense of significance. He puts it this way: "Success commonly means using your knowledge and experience to satisfy yourself with fame and fortune. Significance, however, means the same knowledge and experience to serve others—that is, to change lives."[3]

· I think Buford is just articulating what most people discover anyway as they get older—the definition of success changes. When you are 4 years old, success is not peeing your pants; when you are 14, success is having friends; when you are 24, success is having a spouse; when you are 34, success is making money. By the time you are 74, success is having a spouse, then when you are 84, success is having friends. And when you are 94? Success is not peeing your pants.

SUCCESS = TO USE OUR KNOWLEDGE AND EXPERIENCE TO CHANGE THE LIVES OF OTHERS. GAINING A SENSE OF SIGNIFICANCE IS MERELY A BY-PRODUCT.

Although I whole-heartedly agree with what Buford says, I define success a little differently in the first place. Success, for me, would actually be the same definition he used for significance: to use our knowledge and experience to change the lives of others. Gaining a sense of significance is merely a by-product.

None of this means that we should not continue on our career path or continue to earn a salary but that we should find others in whom we can invest along the way. For others of us, our real passions—the ones that bring that sense of satisfaction or significance—lay beyond our career. It is the reason our church has literally hundreds of volunteers that give countless hours to serve others, with often no earthly reward whatsoever. In fact, if it were not for these people, Church of the Rock would not even exist. They are the people leading weekly neighbourhood Bible studies, marriage ministry courses, children's Sunday school classes, youth or young adult groups, prayer ministry, prison ministry, inner city outreaches, choir, and the list goes on and on. They have tapped into their higher purpose and pursue it with a passion.

Jesus is an interesting example of this. The very first thing He did was gather a dozen men around Him to train. He took these astoundingly average people, who history would never ever have noticed, and used them to change the world. He spent the vast majority of his three and a half years of ministry pouring His life into these twelve men. The rest of His ministry was almost secondary. Without the legacy that the remaining eleven disciples carried on after His death, Jesus' influence would have died at the cross with Him.

Jesus was a revolutionary, not a radical. If he was a lone radical throwing a wrench into the religious status quo of His day, then the plan to kill Him off would have been a good one. But that was not who Jesus was. He had come to start a revolution, which required raising up those who would carry it on after His departure. Jesus' mission was counter-intuitive on numerous levels. In most Cinderella-type stories, the unlikely hero is beloved by the end, not hated. In any Chuck Norris-type action movie, it is the villain who dies at the end, not the hero. Jesus turned the typical narrative on its head. He explains it to His disciples this way:

> *Then they began to question among themselves, which of them it was who would do this thing. Now there was also a dispute among them, as to which of them should be considered the greatest. And He said to them, "The kings of the Gentiles exercise lordship over them, and those who exercise authority over them are called 'benefactors.' But not so among you; on*

the contrary, he who is greatest among you, let him be as the younger, and he who governs as he who serves. For who is greater, he who sits at the table, or he who serves? Is it not he who sits at the table? Yet I am among you as the One who serves."

LUKE 22:23–27

I am not sure they understood it right then, but eventually they did—the things in life that really matter and have lasting significance are the ways we serve others and help them become everything they were meant to be. Jesus took eleven below-average individuals (Judas didn't make the cut) and made world-changing champions out of them. And they, in turn, raised up others after them, and the revolution has continued in a like manner for 2,000 years.

Those of us who have reached middle age should already have a younger person (or several) that we mentor and pour our lives into. Our greatest legacy will not be what we accomplish but what others accomplish after us. We need to adjust our thinking as to what truly makes our life of value. Each and every one of us has a God-given destiny, a destiny that goes far beyond fame and fortune. Some just haven't discovered it yet.

Chapter Three

Begin at the End

The highest reward for man's toil is not what he gets for it,
but what he becomes by it.

— John Ruskin

ALFRED NOBEL WAS born in Stockholm, Sweden, in 1833. His
father, Immanuel Nobel, was the inventor of plywood, and
subsequently, the family became quite wealthy. Growing up with
some degree of privilege, when Alfred was eighteen he went to the
United States to study chemistry. Besides being a trained chemist,
Alfred was an avid reader of literature and was fluent in English,
German, French, Swedish and Russian. He returned to Sweden after
the bankruptcy of their family business and devoted himself to the
study of explosives, especially the safe manufacture and use of nitro-
glycerine. Alfred's business boomed and once again the family was on
an economic upswing. However, in 1864, tragedy struck the Nobel
family. An explosion at their factory killed five people, among them,
Alfred's younger brother Emil.

Though Alfred deeply mourned the loss of his brother, he dealt
with it by burying himself in his work. Far from letting the explosion
slow him down, within only a month he organized other factories to
manufacture explosives. In 1867, Alfred invented a new and safer-to-
handle explosive he named *dynamite*. He became famous for his
invention of dynamite, yet many people did not intimately know

Alfred Nobel. He was a painfully quiet man who did not like a lot of pretense or show. He had very few friends and never married. Though he recognized the destructive power of dynamite, Alfred believed it was a harbinger of peace. Alfred told Bertha von Suttner, an advocate for world peace,

> My factories may make an end of war sooner than your congresses. The day when two army corps can annihilate each other in one second, all civilized nations, it is to be hoped, will recoil from war and discharge their troops.[1]

At the time, Alfred honestly did not see how misguided his thinking was. He would not see peace in his time, and in fact, his invention revolutionized modern warfare.

In 1888, his brother Ludwig Nobel passed away. A French newspaper mistook the news as the death of Alfred and printed an obituary condemning him for his invention of dynamite. The article stated, "The merchant of death is dead," and went on to say, "Dr. Alfred Nobel, who became rich by finding ways to kill more people faster than ever before, died yesterday."[2] Alfred was heartbroken. This was not at all how he saw himself and certainly not the legacy he wanted to leave behind. He did not want to be remembered this way.

This mistaken identity presented him with a unique opportunity that few, if any, ever get. How many people get to see their obituary before they die? Alfred decided to rewrite his. Nobel changed his last will and testament and set aside the bulk of his estate to establish the Nobel Prizes. The prizes would be awarded annually, without distinction of nationality. The five original Nobel Prizes were for Physics, Chemistry, Physiology or Medicine, Literature, and the Nobel Peace Prize, probably the most prestigious humanitarian award of all time.

Alfred Nobel died of a stroke on 10 December 1896, in Italy. He left 31 million kronor to fund the prizes, which would equal 186 million US dollars today. Nobody remembers Alfred Nobel as the "Merchant of Death" but for his extraordinary contribution to the betterment of mankind.

I believe every one of us has the opportunity to write our own obituary. I like to tell people to plan their funerals now. Oh, I don't mean the casket and the flowers and the obligatory luncheon sandwiches with the crusts cut off. What I do mean is, plan what you would like people to say about you after you are gone. What people say about you at your funeral is typically representative of the impact you made on your world.

As I mentioned in the introduction, I am often the last person people see (figuratively) as they are being lowered into the ground to leave this celestial orb. I have come to the conclusion that the money you made, the car you drove and the house you lived in mean nothing once you are dead. There will be plenty time for your family to fight over your car and your house and your jewellery as you are still cooling the grave. No, the only thing that really matters at the time of departure is the difference we make in the lives of others.

WHAT PEOPLE SAY ABOUT YOU AT YOUR FUNERAL IS TYPICALLY REPRESENTATIVE OF THE IMPACT YOU MADE ON YOUR WORLD.

Goodkind said "the universe will go on indifferent to our brief existence."[3] Yes, it will go on, but not indifferently. Everything we do matters; our very purpose in life is to make a difference. Ours is not likely to be on the scale of Alfred Nobel, but that is not the point. What matters is that the world is a better place because we, too, existed for *a greater purpose*. For most of us that will mean a handful who are better people because they knew us. That is our true legacy.

In Steven Covey's brilliant *7 Habits of Highly Effective People*, he calls this principle "beginning with the end in mind."[4] He builds a convincing case that everything is created twice—first in a conceptual way, and then in a literal way. No reputable carpenter would start building a home without first creating it on paper. It must first be created on paper and tweaked possibly hundreds of times before construction starts. Using the plan or blueprint of the finished drawing, he begins with the end in mind. Will it look exactly like the drawing? Usually very close. There will be unforeseen conditions along the way that will determine changes. Maybe suppliers cannot get a certain type or colour of material. Alterations can be made along the way, but at the end of the day, chances are that house is going to look pretty much like the drawing.

One story I like to tell is of the carpenter who worked for a home builder his whole career. At the very end of a project, the company owner came to him and said, "This was the last house we are going to build, since it is time for me to retire. But I have a big surprise for you. For all your faithful service over the years, I am giving this house to you."

"Oh!" responded the surprised carpenter.

His boss was a little disappointed with the response and said, "You don't seem very excited. I am giving you this beautiful brand new home!"

Finally the carpenter admitted, "Well, it's just that if I had known I was building it for myself, I would have put more nails in it."

Our life is our own. It is the only one we get and what we do with it matters for eternity. Some of us need to put more nails in it—more thought, more effort, more planning as to what we want it to look like when we are finished. If we do not begin at the end, there is no telling what we might finish with.

When we were kids, our neighbours at the lake had the biggest cottonwood tree you have ever seen. It was probably six feet across at the base and towered into the clouds. Four or five of us boys decided we needed to build a sky fortress. It was the middle of the week and both dads were at work until the weekend, so they had no idea what we were planning. For a ladder we simply found different lengths of two-by-four boards and nailed them to the side of the tree trunk. Like Jack climbing the beanstalk, we just kept going up until we reached the branches. They were the size of regular trees themselves.

Because we were just kids and had no access to supplies, we crawled under the cottage to see what was there. Good fortune had smiled upon us, as there was a stack of uniformly sized panels ready for the picking. They were small enough to carry up the ladder but big enough to build a platform and walls. We divided into teams— one team to carry the panels up and the other team to build the fortress.

I was part of the construction squad. As the panels came up, I nailed them down to a limb. If there was another branch nearby, I put the panel upright and made a wall. We just kept on building until we ran out of material, since the tree had no shortage of branches. The fortress went here and there, up and down and all over the place. We left openings for windows and doors to access branches we would want to climb out on as a lookout.

We were going to post the requisite "No girls allowed" sign but instead decided that if you were brave enough to climb that precarious and dangerously high ladder, you were welcome to join us. Only my tomboy cousin Lori was able to make the ascent.

I could not have been more proud. It was a true work of art, and to think the whole thing practically designed itself! It was easily the most fun thing we did that summer. However, the party only lasted until Friday night, when our dads came back down for the weekend. As we proudly displayed our handiwork to our fathers, imagine our surprise when they did not share our enthusiasm for the sky fortress.

At the time I did not understand their anger, but now as a father myself, I get it. First, it was perhaps the ugliest thing you have ever seen; built willy-nilly in every direction. Second, at thirty feet above the ground, it was a deathtrap waiting for a disaster to happen. We were very fortunate that nobody fell or got hurt. Finally, that stack of neatly piled building material under the cottage? Those were the window shutters for closing up the cottage for winter. Who knew? Crestfallen, we watched as our dads ran a ladder up the side of the tree to retrieve the shutters and pulled out the enormously dangerous ladder that ran up the trunk. What we had hoped would be a playhouse to last a lifetime existed for less than a week.

At the risk of sounding critical, I have seen many people build their life just like that tree house—carelessly, randomly and even dangerously. If we don't at least to some degree *begin at the end,* we will merely follow the route of least resistance. Just as we kids built along the path of the tree branches, many just let situations and circumstances determine their direction in life. This is not to say that our situations do not play an important role. God not only uses circumstances, but I believe He often sends them our way to direct our path. I have an entire chapter coming up on that. What I am saying is that we do not want to leave the broad strokes to chance. We need to decide what kind of person we want to be and what kind of legacy we want to leave behind and then begin to live out of that vision we have of ourselves.

I remember a man in our church coming to see me one day. He was about thirty years old at the time and going nowhere with his life. He bounced from job to job and had no clear direction. He was married and already had four children, so I guess he knew how to do something well. He was actually very bright and had an engaging personality. He asked if I would pray with him, as he was out of work again and needed a job in a hurry. Before I prayed, I asked him what he wanted to do with his life. He answered, "I want to be a nothing for Jesus."

I think I knew what he was trying to say. He was trying to be humble and submissive to God's plan for his life, but I could not help think "being a nothing" was a pretty weak goal. So I told him so, and instead of allowing me to help him redirect his vision for his life, he argued the point with me. In the end he didn't want prayer from me. He told me I didn't understand his heart and he could work it out on his own. That was fine; it was his life and he could do with it what he wanted. I watched as he continued drifting from job to job, struggling financially, began drinking and eventually left the church and his family. I would hear about him from time to time as he continued to bounce from career to career and woman to woman.

Then one day, out of the blue, he called me up to tell me he was getting married again. I had not seen him for years and did my best to give him my thinly veiled "insincere" congratulations. Then, as I listened most incredulously, he told me I was the best pastor he had ever had and wanted to know if I would perform his marriage. Of course, it was not something I was willing to do. I knew his first wife and had watched his kids grow up with a deadbeat father. I am not sure why he thought I would endorse this new union, but at any rate I politely declined. I am not sure if he got married or not, since I did not get an invitation.

As I hung up the phone that day my thoughts went back to the day in my office two decades ago: "I want to be a nothing for Jesus." Unfortunately, he succeeded.

When I was in my early twenties and attending university, I met another A-type personality named Jim. We had a lot in common, as we were both ambitious, aggressive, entrepreneurial types who annoyed almost everybody around us. One evening at a frat house party, we became engaged in one of those endless late night conversations that move from the practical everyday pursuits of life to the lofty philosophical possibilities of the future. The discussion went many different directions, but at the end of the night there was a pivotal moment, at least so it seems in retrospect. As we parted company we shook hands and made a pact that in twenty years, long after graduation, we would meet again and we would be rich and famous. I know, ridiculous youthful fantasy and delusions of grandeur.

After graduation we only lived an hour apart but we never met up again, even though we were both aware of the other's career progression since we had mutual friends. Almost twenty years to the date, he had become an extremely successful and expansive farmer who was on the cutting edge of the industry. I was pastoring Church of the Rock and by that time our television program was being carried coast to coast across the nation of Canada. I was walking through a downtown shopping mall in Winnipeg when I came face to face with my old friend. The reunion had only lasted three minutes when he said, "I made $600,000 last year."

I responded in surprise, "$600,000?"

"Well, I had to pay taxes on it," he provisioned. I started to laugh.

"I've got a nationally televised TV program," I shamelessly countered, embarrassed to tell him how much money I had made last year. Then I asked him, "Do you remember that pact we made in university that in twenty years we would be rich and famous?"

Without a moment of hesitation he said, "Of course, I do."

"Well," I said, "It has come to pass. You're rich . . . and I'm famous!"

We both had a good laugh, but it was absolutely true. And since that time he has continued to quietly prosper and I have continued to loudly grow more and more well-known. The story is funny, but it is still a testimony to the incredible power of beginning at the end and living toward it. Again, what does that amazing text in Philippians chapter three say?

> *Brethren, I do not count myself to have apprehended; but one thing I do, forgetting those things which are behind and reaching forward to those things which are ahead, I press toward the <u>goal</u> for the prize of the upward call of God in Christ Jesus.*
>
> PHILIPPIANS 3:13–14, *emphasis added*

For the record, I do not consider the goals we made that night particularly noble in the greater scheme of life, but that is not the point I am making. The point is, when we begin at the end there is really nothing that we cannot accomplish. That is why it is important to focus on the things that really matter, things that have eternal value and make our world a better place.

Let me try to put this in the proper perspective. Whenever I see the bumper sticker "He who has the most toys when he dies, wins!" I always think I would like to design one that says, "He who has the most toys when he dies, STILL DIES!" Maybe they would sell like hotcakes and I could die rich. Or would that contradict everything I am trying to say? The only real treasures we leave behind are the ways that we have improved the lives of the people around us. The only real legacy any of us leaves is how we have impacted our world for the better. Alfred Nobel rewrote his epitaph. We can too. He began with the end in mind.

THE ONLY REAL TREASURES WE LEAVE BEHIND ARE THE WAYS THAT WE HAVE IMPROVED THE LIVES OF THE PEOPLE AROUND US. THE ONLY REAL LEGACY ANY OF US LEAVES IS HOW WE HAVE IMPACTED OUR WORLD FOR THE BETTER.

We rarely think of applying this principle to our epitaph. But I think we should. Imagine how you would like to be remembered after you are gone, and then start living into that vision now while you are still alive. That's how you write your own eulogy. That's exactly what Alfred Nobel did after he had a premature look at his epitaph.

One of my favourite jokes is about the three men who were discussing this very subject. They each pondered what they would like others to say as they stared into their caskets.

The first man said, "I would like them to say he was a good husband and a loving father."

The second man said, "I would want them to say he was a brilliant surgeon who saved many lives."

The third man said, "I would like them to gaze into the coffin and say, 'LOOK, HE'S MOVING!'"

The Apostle Paul addresses it this way,

According to the grace of God which was given to me, as a wise master builder I have laid the foundation, and another builds on it. But let each one take heed how he builds on it. For no other foundation can anyone lay than that which is laid, which is Jesus Christ. Now if anyone builds on this foundation with gold, silver, precious stones, wood, hay, straw, each one's work will become clear; for the Day will declare it, because it will be revealed by fire; and the fire will test each one's work, of what sort it is. If anyone's work which he has built on it endures, he will receive a reward. If anyone's work is burned, he will suffer loss; but he himself will be saved, yet so as through fire.

1 CORINTHIANS 3:10–15

Simply put, everything we do in life can be categorized as either wood, hay and straw, or gold, silver and precious stones. When we get to heaven, our works will be tried by fire. How are the deeds of wood, hay and straw going to make out? They will be burned up, lost, counted as worthless. Now, if we know Christ, we still make it to heaven irrespective of our works. However, only the deeds of gold, silver and precious stone will remain and determine some apparent level of heavenly reward. It should not be terribly hard to figure out that wood, hay and straw are the many, many pointless things we do in life that have no eternal value. The time spent watching television, playing video games or waxing the car has no eternal value. Only the things that influence and affect others have eternal value. Jesus put it this way, *"For whoever gives you a cup of water to drink in My name, because you belong to Christ, assuredly, I say to you, he will by no means lose his reward"* (Mark 9:41).

A few years ago I conducted a funeral for a man I had met on only one occasion, standing in the checkout line at Walmart. So, I didn't really know him at all. Gathered with his family to plan the service, I asked his three sons to name all of their father's positive qualities. They sat there in deaf silence like I had asked them to give me the square root of 5,625 (it's 75, by the way). Finally, after prodding them with words like kind, generous, loving, caring, funny, industrious, hardworking, one of them said, "Yeah, hardworking!" Yup, they all agreed, he was hardworking. Sixty-eight years of life, and all they could come up with was "hardworking." Now, I know there was more to this man than what his three sons could come up with during their moment of grief. But I will never know, as that is all they gave me. Imagine my challenge of building an entire memorial service around the theme of "a hardworking man, who shopped at Walmart, who will be dearly missed."

As I conducted the funeral, all I could think about was that old story about Sophie Jones. Sophie had lived to be 100 years old and the local newspaper thought it would be nice to do a piece on her. By default, the sports reporter got assigned to the story, and he could find nothing on her. She was never married, never had a traffic ticket, didn't belong to any clubs, and had few friends and no enemies. In the end he wrote a simple epitaph:

> Here lie the bones of Sophie Jones;
> For her life held no terrors.
> She lived an old maid,
>
> She died an old maid.
> No hits, no runs, and no errors (heirs).

Try doing a funeral with that going through your already easily-distracted mind! As I said, I am actually quite sure there was more to this man than that, but you get the point. The memories people have of us after we are gone are a pretty fair reflection of who we were. Fortunately for us, they mostly only talk about the good stuff.

Planning one's funeral really is a valuable way to script one's life. Very few of us are going to be the next Alfred Nobel, Martin Luther King Jr. or Mother Teresa (the latter two are Nobel Peace Prize laureates). But every one of us can leave a lasting significant contribution to our world if we *begin at the end.*

Chapter Four

A Blast from the Past

The past is a foreign country; they do things differently there.
— Leslie Poles Hartley

I GREW UP in a Roman Catholic family of six kids: four brothers and twin sisters. I guess you would consider my parents moderates. I wouldn't trade growing up in a big family for anything. It has provided me with a lifetime of sermon illustrations. When I tell stories from the pulpit about growing up, my poor mother, who has been with us since the church began, is in a perpetual state of shock. "Where was I when all this was happening?" she will ask me almost every week. The good news is she just doesn't remember; the bad news is it really did happen.

Putting the past behind us is one of the great keys to moving forward into life's purposes. Those who continue to dwell on the hurts, habits and hang-ups of the past will be perpetually bound by the limitations of the past.

The apostle Paul knew something about this. He was formerly known as Saul of Tarsus. He was a murderer and a persecutor of the church. However, after his dramatic conversion experience on the road to Damascus, he became the champion of the gospel. He had to live down the reputation he had acquired in his past in order to fulfill his future destiny. *"But they were hearing only, 'He who formerly persecuted us now preaches the faith which he once tried to destroy'"*

53

(Galatians 1:23). Somehow Paul managed to break free of who he was to become the man he was meant to be.

In Philippians 3:12–14, he gives us the secret.

> *Not that I have already attained, or am already perfected; but I press on, that I may lay hold of that for which Christ Jesus has also laid hold of me. Brethren, I do not count myself to have apprehended; <u>but one thing I do, forgetting those things which are behind</u> and reaching forward to those things which are ahead, I press toward the goal for the prize of the upward call of God in Christ Jesus.*

Clearly, the starting point is forgetting those things which are behind.

PUTTING THE PAST BEHIND US IS ONE OF THE GREAT KEYS TO MOVING FORWARD INTO LIFE'S PURPOSES.

My brother Tod is just sixteen months behind me in age. We shared a room our whole lives and could pretty much finish each other's sentences. He is easily my single biggest source of sermon illustrations. He was always into mischief of one sort or another and he was the brother in every big family that drives your father crazy. When I tell stories of my past, I have found it very convenient to assign even the ones I was guilty of to my brother Tod. He will often hear them on TV and phone me up to object that it was actually me that did some terrible deed, not him. It doesn't really matter, though, because his reputation is such that no one will believe him.

In the mid-1970s, when I was around eighteen years old and Tod was around seventeen, he went out and bought an old milk truck for $600. It was one of those square delivery trucks with the sliding side doors, not unlike what UPS uses today. The difference was that this was a piece of junk and had outlived its useful service. Tod's plan was to convert it to a motorhome and prowl North America looking for adventure. He asked for my help, as I was clearly the smart one, and the conversion began. We wired the back for 110V power. It had lights and a heater. We ran an extension cord to our parent's house and now he was ready to poach hydro from any receptacle he could find. Next, we lined the entire living quarters with orange and green shag carpet that had come out of our basement family room. It was a thing of beauty.

There was only one slight problem. The only time the beast ever ran was the day he bought it. He drove it into the driveway and it promptly quit running, never to fire up again. We messed with the motor for days but didn't really know what we were doing, so we never got it going. Month after month, this hideous eyesore sat in our driveway, until one day my dad could not stand it any longer. Summoning the two of us, he informed us that the "milk truck" needed to be gone by the end of the week.

Tod objected, "It's not a milk truck, it's a motorhome."

My father's measured response was, "I don't care what you call it. It needs to be out of the driveway by the end of the week."

For some reason the lot fell to me to try to sell it. I placed an ad in the *Winnipeg Free Press* classifieds, since Al Gore had not yet invented the internet. The ad read, "Motorhome, excellent condition $300. May need tune-up." The ad had to be short because you paid by the word. That week we only had one call, but at least the guy showed up to look at it. As he came up to the front door, my first tip-off that this might not go as planned was the way he was dressed. He was wearing early Salvation Army thrift shop. At any rate, he loved the "motorhome" and said he wanted it.

I told him, "You do realize that it doesn't actually run?"

To which he responded, "That's fine, I just want to curl up in it right where it is."

It was then that it dawned on me that a homeless man had showed up, hoping to live in the milk truck on our driveway. I wasn't the sharpest tool in the shed, but I was pretty sure the only thing worse than having an old milk truck in the driveway was having a milk truck with a homeless man living in it in the driveway.

Having reached our deadline, my father told us Friday morning on the way to work that the milk truck needed to be out of the driveway by the time he got home that evening. Tod objected, "It's not a milk truck, it's a motorhome." This time my father said nothing and headed off to work.

This many years later I can't remember which one of us was responsible for what happened next, but I will blame it on my brother Tod. We went around to the back of the house and dismantled the fence. We then pushed the milk truck around the house and into the back yard. We did our best to reassemble the fence, but it looked pretty crooked. But whoever looks at the back yard fence, anyway?

I don't ever remember seeing my father looking as happy as he did when he arrived home that evening. It made our hearts feel proud that we were able to do this thing for our dad. "Boys," he said, "I don't care what you have done with the milk truck; I am just glad it is gone. Thank you." For some strange reason, Tod did not correct him and tell him it was actually a motorhome. The whole time I was thinking to myself how glad I was that he "didn't care what we had done with it." But I, too, kept silent.

The next morning was Saturday and my father slept in till 9 AM. With his bedroom facing the back yard, he went to the window to throw open the curtains to greet the day. Instead, he was greeted by the sight of a broken down milk truck and a broken down fence. I will never forget the growl that awakened me that morning. The sound of a grizzly bear in the wild would not do it justice. Turns out, he did care what we had done with the milk truck. Who would have thought? That day we paid the wrecker twenty-five dollars to tow away the motorhome and that was the last we saw of it. We never did get the fence fixed. It was a minor detail in the greater scheme of things.

There is a point to all of this. We all have a milk truck in the back yard of our lives. We all have things that are unsightly, unhelpful and unwanted, and yet they somehow have a way of raising their ugly heads when we at last think they are gone. Paul said we need to learn to *"forget the things which are behind"* (Philippians 3:13). We need to figure out what things in our past need to be hauled off to the dump, never to be seen again. On our own, we are not likely to succeed, but when Jesus comes into our lives everything changes. *"Therefore, if anyone is in Christ, he is a new creation; old things have passed away; behold, all things have become new"* (2 Corinthians 5:17).

WE ALL HAVE A MILK TRUCK IN THE BACK YARD OF OUR LIVES. WE ALL HAVE THINGS THAT ARE UNSIGHTLY, UNHELPFUL AND UNWANTED, AND YET THEY SOMEHOW HAVE A WAY OF RAISING THEIR UGLY HEADS WHEN WE AT LAST THINK THEY ARE GONE.

Serge LeClerc had a very inauspicious start to life. He was born in an abandoned building in Montreal, a product of rape. There is actually no record of his birth at all. His mother was a thirteen-year-old Cree girl who had run away from home. His young mother took them to live in Toronto's inner city. With no positive life experience herself and little in the way of parenting skills, she left Serge to find his own way in life. For the most part he raised himself.

By age eight, he was admitted to a residential school. Though for the first time in his young life he had a proper roof over his head and food on the table, other perils lurked in the corridors of the residential school. He, like many others, began to be sexually and physically abused. Young Serge concluded that life on the streets was more appealing and he ran away, living in abandoned buildings and eating out of garbage bins.

Over the next few years, it was a game of cat and mouse with authorities. Each time he ended up back in the residential school, he become more unruly and violent. As the abuse at the school continued, Serge was no longer passive but pulled out a knife and stabbed one of his abusers. He was shuffled around between foster homes and youth detention centres. Psychiatric specialists labelled him as "brain damaged," which at the time he thought was "pretty cool" and gave him licence to act however he pleased. No one could see any hope for the future of this young man. He was considered incorrigible and beyond help.

By age fifteen, Serge was back on his own, leading one of the largest, toughest street gangs in Toronto. He carried a gun, ran alcohol stills and extortion rackets, and wore his label of "brain damaged" as a badge of honour. In the sixties, he was one of the pioneers in the lucrative business of dealing drugs. Still in his teens, Serge carried a roll of one-hundred-dollar bills and once walked into an auto dealer and bought a car with cash. Over the next twenty years, he became a fixture in Canada's criminal underworld and rose to the top of one of the nation's most notorious crime families.

The good times never really lasted very long, however, as he was never more than half a step in front of the law. In and out of prison, he began to do "life on the instalment plan," as he called it. He spent more time in jail than he did on the streets, and he did much of his business from behind bars. In 1984, Serge landed the big one and began a nine-year term for a $40 million drug bust. Because of an incident with a guard, he was put in solitary confinement and sat alone and finally broken, waiting to be transferred to a maximum security prison.

One day, as Serge Leclerc languished away in abject solitude, he received a rare visitor. The volunteer prison worker shared the gospel with Serge and told him that God had a plan for his life. At that time he could only see himself as completely, totally and utterly useless and had thoughts of taking his own life. The volunteer told him he actually had a choice. He could believe that he was an animal that walked on two legs, with no purpose, or he could believe that he was created by God with a soul and that he was of great value and had a purpose in life.

Seven months later, he watched a nineteen-year-old man commit suicide in the next cell. The young man was there because of drug use from Serge's own lab and drug dealers. He thought about what the volunteer had said months earlier. He attended a prison chapel service and asked for a Bible. They gave him a Gideon Bible. As he read the New Testament, he was taken by the story of Jesus and His disciples. He could relate to the story about a gang leader and his gang members. He understood completely why they hid when Jesus was crucified but did not know why they emerged from hiding and risked the same fate. Then it dawned on him. He realized that these men had discovered something. Truth! Only the truth was worth suffering persecution and even death.

So one morning in 1985, Serge bowed down on the cold cement floor of his cell and received Jesus Christ as his personal Lord and Saviour. In that moment everything changed. Serge Leclerc became a new person. He became a model prisoner. The Word of God became his new blueprint to reinvent himself. He became the first convict in a Canadian prison to complete a university degree while serving his sentence. He graduated with honours, completing a degree in sociology and social work from the University of Waterloo. When he got out of prison in 1988, he continued to try to seek God's purpose for his life. In 2000, Serge Leclerc received a full government pardon, which required an act of Parliament to be granted. Never before had a national crime figure been granted a national pardon. Parliamentarians credited his work with Crimestoppers as the reason. Police chiefs and RCMP inspectors testified to the government that he was a changed man.

Eventually Serge became the regional director of Teen Challenge in Saskatchewan and one of Canada's most in-demand speakers. In November 2007, the people of Saskatoon elected Serge a member of the Saskatchewan Legislature. He had been once classified as one of the most violent men in the Canadian penitentiary system, but he become one of the nation's most respected public servants. As Serge liked to say, "Never before in the history of North America has someone gone from lawbreaker to lawmaker."* If Serge Leclerc can get free from the baggage of his past, then there is hope for anyone.

---

* There is a sad ending to the Serge Leclerc story. In the spring of 2010, the CBC received a package of audio recordings alleging drug use and gay sex by Leclerc while he served as an MLA. He insisted he was innocent and that someone was trying to set him up. In September 2010, he resigned his seat in the Saskatchewan Legislature so he could clear his name. However, only a month later he was diagnosed with stomach and colon cancer and by April 16, 2011, he passed away, exactly one year to the date on which the CBC recordings became public. None of this changes the point I am making. I had the opportunity of personally meeting Serge and hearing him speak. He was clearly a changed man and no longer the hardened criminal mind he once was. It is tragic that he died before he had a chance to clearly set the record straight. I have to think that somehow in God's sovereignty there is a point even to that.

Chapter Five

So Long, Sin City

So long Sin City, so long,
you've seen me crying
while I know this life was lonely, ah yea
I know this life was sweet,
goodbye my love, goodbye
I am leaving the table
let the drinks, let the drinks and the cards flow
let them flow like Jesus' blood

— Slash, of Guns and Roses[1]

THE SLOGAN THAT the marketing gurus came up with for Las Vegas is "What happens in Vegas, stays in Vegas." It is quite clever, really. It appeals to the universal desire for consequence-free sinning. Do what you please, sin all you want, push the boundaries of your own sense of human decency and it will all return to normal when you get home. The reality is somewhat different. The only thing that stays in Vegas is your money. It is the one place on earth that you can arrive driving a $50,000 Cadillac and return home in a $250,000 Greyhound bus. The consequences of sin hang on us like a cheap suit. A bad trip to Vegas could see you take home AIDS or another sexually transmitted disease, an empty bank account, a loan from a shady character named Knuckles, a gambling habit, a porn addiction . . . the list goes on and on.

As stated in the last chapter, one of the biggest challenges in moving forward in life is getting free from the baggage of the past. The single greatest bondage of the past is sin. Nothing has the power to hold us captive like sin, both ours and the sin of others. Unfortunately, the word "sin" is being written out of the English lexicon. People don't like being told they are sinners and they don't like being told what they do is sin. They prefer words like "alternative lifestyle." Instead of calling abortion "murder," we call it "choice." Instead of calling homosexuality "sin," we call it a "genetically predisposed sexual orientation." We have no end of justifications for our behaviour and do not feel there should be any consequences for them.

There is a joke about Bill Clinton dying and arriving at the Pearly Gates. St. Peter asks him if he committed any sins while on earth. Bill asks what he means by sin. Peter responds, "You know, what bad things did you do on earth?"

Clinton thought a bit and answered, "Well, I smoked marijuana, but I did not inhale. So you can't hold that against me. I was unfaithful in my marriage, but 'I did not have sexual relations with that woman.' And I lied, but I did not commit perjury. So if you ask me, I think I am good to go."

After several moments St. Peter replied, "Okay, if that is how you want to play it, here's the deal. We'll send you someplace where it is very hot, but we won't call it 'Hell.' You'll be there for an indefinite period of time, but we won't call it 'eternity.' But don't abandon all hope because you will only be there till it freezes over."

I am not evil, just misunderstood.
Well okay, I am misunderstood and evil.

— Unknown

The word "sin" has become so unpopular that many well-known preachers have stopped using it altogether. I remember watching CNN's Larry King interviewing a well-known preacher a few years back. Here is an excerpt straight from the transcript:[2]

> KING: How about issues that the church has feelings about? Abortion? Same-sex marriages?
>
> PREACHER: Yeah. You know what, Larry? I don't go there. I just...
>
> KING: You have thoughts, though.
>
> PEACHER: I have thoughts. I just, you know, I don't think that a same-sex marriage is the way God intended it to be. I don't think abortion is the best. I think there are other, you know, a better way to live your life. But I'm not going to condemn those people. I tell them all the time our church is open for everybody.
>
> KING: You don't call them sinners?
>
> PREACHER: I don't.
>
> KING: Is that a word you don't use?
>
> PREACHER: "I don't use it. I never thought about it. But I probably don't. But most people already know what they're doing wrong. When I get them to church I want to tell them that you can change. There can be a difference in your life. So I don't go down the road of condemning."

A preacher that doesn't use the word "sin"? Interesting! My intent here is to avoid criticism of this individual and instead focus on the concept. I understand where this preacher is coming from and what he is trying to accomplish, but we have a fundamental disagreement. I do not believe people in our day and age know what sin is. How could they? If they don't read the Bible and preachers have stopped talking about it, how would they know what sin is? The Bible uses the word directly 830 times, and indirectly, thousands more. But today's preachers are afraid to use the word for risk of offending people. As a consequence, the people they don't want to offend are hopelessly bound by the sins of their past. We think we will lose them if we talk about sin, but in fact we are losing them because we do not. It is virtually impossible to convince people that they are in need of a Saviour if they cannot first see that they have a problem. The universal problem is sin. It always has been, always will be.

I DO NOT BELIEVE PEOPLE IN OUR DAY AND AGE KNOW WHAT SIN IS. HOW COULD THEY? IF THEY DON'T READ THE BIBLE AND PREACHERS HAVE STOPPED TALKING ABOUT IT, HOW WOULD THEY KNOW WHAT SIN IS?

A study of primitive cultures reveals almost every civilization has had some sort of religious observance that was meant to try to atone for the guilt of sin. For many, it was some sort of sacrifice. Muslims bow toward Mecca five times daily. Hindus will travel hundreds of miles to the Ganges River to try to wash their sins away. All humans have a deep rooted sense of their own sinfulness but often do not connect the dots to the grief and calamity which comes as a consequence. What heartache can be attributed to lust, greed, wrath, sloth, pride, envy, and gluttony—the seven deadly sins? The answer is calculable. For us as a culture to sanitize sin as a 'lifestyle choice' is nothing short of disastrous. The good news of course, is that this is exactly what Jesus came for, to remedy the problem. What did the bumper sticker say again? If Jesus is the answer, then what is the question?

I read an article on the CNN Belief Blogs recently about how the church is doing a poor job of reaching the next generation, especially young adults. The author, Rachel Held Evans, claimed that,

> Young adults perceive evangelical Christianity to be too political, too exclusive, old-fashioned, unconcerned with social justice and hostile to lesbian, gay, bisexual and transgender people. . . . research shows that young evangelicals often feel they have to choose between their intellectual integrity and their faith, between science and Christianity, between compassion and holiness and finally that the evangelical obsession with sex can make Christian living seem like little more than sticking to a list of rules then being a safe place for which they can ask tough questions and wrestle with their doubts. [3]

I found myself agreeing with much of her conclusion but wondered about the question of sin and how young adults felt about hearing it from the pulpit. I gathered a group of a couple of dozen young people after church one Sunday and asked them that very question. The group consisted of lifelong Christians, brand new believers and everything in between. Overwhelmingly, they expressed that if the church did not address sin from the pulpit, they would not know what it is. They explained how they are not told in school, in movies, on TV, through pop culture and, for many of them, not even at home. Where would one hear about the dangers of sin anywhere today? Every type of behaviour is tolerated in virtually any setting. If the church becomes silent on the subject, then there will be no voice left. Please do not misunderstand what I am saying. I do not advocate the old-school hellfire and brimstone preaching that puts people into further guilt and fear. I am talking about asking the tough questions in a thoughtful way which ultimately leads people to ask themselves whether they are really living the way they want to or not.

The gospel is actually profoundly simple if one takes the time to try to understand it. Our first father and mother, Adam and Eve, were put on the earth in a pure and sinless state. They lived in paradise. There was no war, no sickness, no sorrow, no poverty, no violence and I guess no mosquitoes. They were naked, and if there were mosquitoes, then that would not be paradise. Exactly how many years ago all this happened is up for debate. Some say 6,000 years ago, while others say tens of thousands of years ago. The 6,000 year thing has always been a big hang-up for some people. For the sake of understanding the gospel, it doesn't really matter. What matters is "what" happened, not "when."

HE COULD HAVE CREATED MAN WITHOUT A FREE WILL. HE COULD HAVE PUT HIM IN A CLOISTERED WORLD WITHOUT TEMPTATION. BUT THEN HE WOULD HAVE ROBOTS ON HIS HANDS, NOT HUMANS.

In Genesis 2, God told Adam not to eat of the fruit of the tree in the midst of the garden. The tree was called the Tree of the Knowledge of Good and Evil. Presumably, Adam and Eve only knew good and not evil. God warned them that in the day that they ate of the tree, they would die. By Genesis 3, they had already eaten. They did not die, at least not physically. They did die, however, spiritually. They were now cut off from God and were run out of the Garden of Eden.

Someone once said that Eve was the first woman in history to eat her family out of house and home. The thing that is crucial to understand is that the spiritual condition of the world drastically changed. The book of Romans puts it this way, *"For as by one man's disobedience many were made sinners, so also by one Man's obedience many will be made righteous"* (Romans 5:19).

Adam and Eve introduced the problem of sin to the human race. Each and every one of us comes into this world as a sinner; we are predisposed to sin. It is just a matter of time before our selfish sinful nature emerges. You see, we are not punished for what Adam and Eve did. That would be a bit unjust. We are punished for our own sin. We did not inherit their damnation, but because we inherited their sin nature, we sin.

> *Therefore, just as through one man sin entered the world, and death through sin, and thus death spread to all men, because all sinned.*
>
> ROMANS 5:12

At about this point the objection always arises, "Well, if God who is all knowing, and He knew Adam and Eve were going to sin, then He set us up to fail." It is true—God did know man would fall. He was the one who put the temptation in the garden in the first place. The short answer to a very complex question is this: He could have created man without a free will. He could have put him in a cloistered world without temptation. But then He would have robots on His hands, not humans. One of the amazing truths of Scripture is that God will always give man the choice to choose Him or reject Him. Even after the return of Christ to the earth for the millennial reign, He will loose Satan from the bottomless pit one more time.

> *And he cast him into the bottomless pit, and shut him up, and set a seal on him, so that he should deceive the nations no more*

till the thousand years were finished. But after these things he
must be released for a little while.

REVELATION 20:3

Why would God do this? To give every person born during that 1,000 years a chance to choose, just like Adam and Eve and just like you and I. It's a tough pill to swallow, but it is the way it is. He's God, we're not. He makes the rules. So, one could argue that God put us into the predicament in the first place (you could argue you it, but you would be wrong). Either way, He was not at all happy with the situation, and He Himself provided the remedy.

Then the Lord saw it, and it displeased Him
That there was no justice.
He saw that there was no man,
And wondered that there was no intercessor;
Therefore His own arm brought salvation for Him;
And His own righteousness, it sustained Him.

ISAIAH 59:15b–16

He sent His Son, Jesus, to the earth to pay the price for man's sinfulness. The death on the cross was to reverse the curse that was brought by Adam and Eve.

For the wages of sin is death, but the gift of God is eternal life
in Christ Jesus our Lord.

ROMANS 6:23

But God demonstrates His own love toward us, in that while
we were still sinners, Christ died for us.

ROMANS 5:8

There is no way to overestimate the importance of the work of the cross. Without it, we are all still dead in our sin and destined for an eternity far worse than anyone could possibly imagine. When Jesus told Nicodemus, *"You must be born again,"* (John 3:7) He was referring to the fact that though he was physically alive, he was spiritually dead. When we accept Christ as our Lord and Saviour, He not only forgives our sin but spiritually regenerates us. In other words, we are "born again" or spiritually reborn. That rebirth changes us from the inside out and we become free from the bondage of sin that has ensnared us for our entire lives. This is why the modern notion that all religions are more or less equal is so patently incorrect. Jesus, and only Jesus, died for the forgiveness of sins. As virtuous as the teaching of other religions are, none of them can address the fundamental problem of our sinfulness. That is why Jesus made the audacious but true claim, *"I am the way, the truth, and the life. No one comes to the Father except through Me"* (John 14:6).

Dear reader, if you have never made a decision to invite Jesus into your life as your Lord and Saviour, I would encourage you to do so, even now. Failure to do so leaves us hopelessly bound to the sins of our past. A simple but sincere prayer to ask Jesus into your heart instantly releases you from the eternal consequence of your past sins. *"Therefore if the Son makes you free, you shall be free indeed"* (John 8:36).

Chapter Six

The Time Machine

My only regret in life is that I am not someone else.

— Woody Allen

AN AMISH FAMILY came to the big city for the very first time. Momma needed some medical care and this was the only place they could get it. After they parked the horse and buggy at a meter, they wandered down the street looking up at the buildings with bewildered awe. Once in the medical centre, Momma wandered into the gift shop while the father and his teenage son stood in front of the elevator door.

"What is that room, Pa?" said the teen.

"Don't rightly know, Son," replied the father.

Just then the doors opened and an old woman with a walker shuffled inside the little room. The doors closed, and three minutes later when they opened again, a gorgeous twenty-four-year-old blond emerged.

The Amish man smiled slightly and said, "Son, go git yer Ma."

As a culture, we are fascinated with time travel. The theme continues to appear in novels, television and movies. The first introduction of the concept in literature was in 1895, with H. G. Wells's novella, *The Time Machine*. This was an entire decade before Einstein had even begun musing about the theoretical possibility in 1905. The first actual working time machine wasn't invented until

1985, when Dr. Emmett Brown came up with the flux capacitor-powered DeLorean. Travelling at a speed of 88 miles per hour, with the application of 1.21 gigawatts of power, time travel became possible.

Or did I only see that in a movie?[1]

What is it that appeals to us about the concept of time travel? Aside from the intrigue of the science fiction, it is the idea that one could actually change their past that has the most allure. Human beings are the only species that experiences the emotion of regret. We all have things in our past that we would give anything to go back in time and change: a life altering accident, a bad financial decision, an ill-spoken word.

> "Does this dress make me look fat?" (Careful, men—the wrong answer could put you on the couch for a week.)

We can all recall countless instances of moments we would like to redo. I have many regretful experiences that still gnaw at my memory today. One in particular occurred one absolutely perfect August long weekend.

We were out on beautiful Lake of the Woods in Ontario for a leisurely boat ride in our pathetic little eighteen-horsepower, thirty-five-year-old fishing boat. Nevertheless, you could not find a more idyllic day to be on the water. It was dead calm and twenty-eight degrees Celsius. Kathy had suggested we take a ride down to a nearby beach. I had something more adventurous in mind. I insisted we should visit the "swinging rope." This was a treacherous spot where someone had hung a rope from a tree that was growing out over top of a rocky cliff. One could jump from the cliff holding onto the rope and swing "safely" out over the rocks and into deep water. The number of people injured there every year was ridiculous. Why a father would take his school-aged kids there is a mystery to me (at least now). At the time, it seemed like a perfect way to spend an afternoon.

We were not there for more than one minute when my seven-year-old daughter got hit in the face by the knot on the end of the rope and knocked out her front tooth. Her adult teeth had just grown in that summer. We had actually never seen her with teeth before, since she had knocked both her baby teeth out in separate accidents as a baby. We spent years waiting for those new teeth to arrive. Finally they did, and now, in an instant, one of them was gone. I spent the next hour futilely diving in the twenty-foot deep water, looking for the missing tooth in hopes that a dentist might be able to re-implant it. I dove till I was physically exhausted and could not dive even one more time. To make matters worse, the boat would not start and we had to hitch a tow from another boater.

During the slow ride home, I looked upon my little daughter's sad, toothless face. That night I had a restless sleep as I continued to dream all night long that I was still diving in those cold deep waters, looking for the tooth. Sure, it was only a tooth and could have been a lot worse, but that one small moment forever altered the trajectory of our life in a number of ways. Since that day we have spent countless hours in dentists' waiting rooms. We spent thousands of dollars on bridges and dental work. There were many uncomfortable nights as the pain from a new dental appliance prevented our little girl—and us—from sleeping. Several times we got a call from the school to come and pick our daughter up as the $800 bridge was once again broken when she was hit by a ball in gym class. The missing tooth caused all the other teeth to become misaligned and required her to wear braces for three years. Now, as a young adult, she must have maxi-facial surgery to implant new bone in the front of her mouth, and eventually she will have an implant. Another five thousand dollars. Needless to say, I wish we had gone to the beach.

It is incredible to me how the small events of our lives can redirect our paths in significant ways. We all have these stories, most much worse than this one. The bigger question is, what are we going to do with it? Are we going to live with a sense of regret and guilt? You cannot go through life thinking, *If only I had done this, if only I had done that*. We are all products of the events of our past. The families that raised us, the people who influenced us and the mistakes made along the way all made a lasting impression on us.

One of my favourite illustrations for this concept is that of the little baby circus elephant. When he was first purchased by the circus, he was a handful. Untrained, he would wander around and get into trouble. The trainers discovered that if they placed a little yellow polypropylene rope around his leg they could keep him tethered. The thing about little baby elephants is that they grow into huge adult elephants. An African male can weigh up to 15,000 pounds. The incredible thing the trainers discovered was that, even though the elephant was full grown, they could put the same little yellow rope around its leg and it would remain tethered. While it could easily have snapped the rope like a piece of thread, it did not. The elephant had become ensnared by the limitations of the past. That is a picture of most every one of us in one way or another. We have past hurts, habits and hang-ups that tether us to our past and restrict our future.

But what if you really could change your past?

> *Therefore, from now on, we regard no one according to the flesh. Even though we have known Christ according to the flesh, yet now we know Him thus no longer. Therefore, if anyone is in Christ, he is a new creation; old things have passed away; behold, all things have become new.*
>
> 2 CORINTHIANS 5:16–17

The Scripture explicitly states that when we are in Christ everything changes. The "old things" have passed away and "all things have become new." That's right, it's incredible—the day after you got saved, you woke up in the morning and the mortgage was paid, the bald spot on the back of your head was gone and your wife looked like Angelina Jolie! Nooooo. The mortgage is still in arrears, you are still using Rogaine and your wife still looks like Phyllis Diller. Everything has changed all right, but all the changes are on the inside not the outside.

Our parents' genetics, our economic status and the schools we attended all conspire together to determine who we are and where we are going. For instance, the dashing young Prince William, Duke of Cambridge, kind of has it made: born into royalty, a handsome lifelong salary courtesy of the British people, and all the best schools. The chances of him ending up on the street are none and zero. Contrast that with another William.

We were in Matamoras, Mexico, ministering in the squatters' village there. A young boy named Guillermo (Spanish for William) emerged one morning from his home, a shanty made of cardboard and discarded tin. He was dirty, hungry and pathetic but he had a sweet disposition and he spent every day hanging out with us. If there were a "continuum of Williams," he would be on the other end of the scale from Prince William. Born into a poor Mexican family, he had never attended school a day in his life because his parents could not afford the requisite uniform to send him to even the free public school.

What did each of these Williams do to deserve their particular lot in life? Nothing! Prince William of Wales was born into the Lucky Sperm Club, as one of my friends indelicately puts it. Prince William of Matamoras, as I dubbed him, was not. They are both products of their past, plain and simple. Are we doomed by fate and chance? Not when we know Christ. We become members of a new royal family.

We become a nation of "kings and priests" the Bible tells us (Revelation 1:6; 5:10). When we find Christ, the limitations and the shackles of the past are lifted. *Old things have passed away.*

In Judges 6 we find Gideon threshing wheat in the bottom of a winepress. Typically, the ancients would thresh wheat on the top of a rise. The wheat would be beaten and then thrown into the air where the wind would blow the chaff away. Because the Midianites had overrun the land and were destroying the Israelite crops, Gideon, for fear of them, was threshing wheat in the windless bottom of the winepress. A pathetic sight, if you think about it. Just then the Angel of the Lord appears and tells Gideon he has been chosen to lead Israel against the Midianites. His response is classic. *"O my Lord, how can I save Israel? Indeed my clan is the weakest in Manasseh, and I am the least in my father's house."* (Judges 6:15)

Gideon played the inferiority card. *Don't you know who I am, Lord? I am the weakest and the least.* In his mind, he was bound by the limitations of the past. But God wouldn't hear any of it—He called him *"a mighty man of valor."* (Judges 6:12). He told him he would *"defeat the Midianites as one man."* (Judges 6:16). Eventually Gideon somehow got hold of it and went out and defeated the Midianites.

I consider Gideon's story to be one of the most instructive lessons anywhere for overcoming the limitations of the past. It is the quintessential example of the battle between how God sees us and how we see ourselves. The war was not on the battlefield but in the mind. Gideon had to change his mindset before he would ever see his God-given destiny unfold.

> *And do not be conformed to this world, but be transformed <u>by the renewing of your mind</u>, that you may prove what is that good and acceptable and perfect will of God.*
>
> ROMANS 12:2, *emphasis added*

"Renewing your mind" simply means reading about and meditating on what God has to say about us from Scripture rather than what our past has been dictating for years. The challenge for most of us is that we focus more on where we have been than on where we are going. Our human nature tends to want to brood about our past hurts and failures. As I like to say: we rehearse it, curse it and nurse it.

REHEARSING THE PAST

When something hurts us deeply, it is admittedly hard to get free of it. We cannot stop thinking about it and we rehearse it over and over again in our mind. Sometimes the painful memories of childhood are right there like they happened yesterday. They were painful the first time, so why would we want to relive them again? I have met eighty-year-old people who have bitter memories that are almost as old as they are, and yet they still carry them. Paul the apostle said, *"One thing I do, forgetting those things which are behind [I reach] forward to those things which are ahead"* (Philippians 3:13).

How do you know if you are rehearsing the past? You need to listen to the things you speak about. *"Out of the abundance of the heart [the] mouth speaks"* (Luke 6:45b). When you find yourself continually talking about a past experience, you are rehearsing it. No amount of discussing it can change what happened. Sure, you cannot forget it entirely, but do you really want to relive it over and over again? When you do, you find yourself trapped in the past.

Some dear people we know had a daughter with Downs Syndrome. She had many health problems and was only supposed to live until she was in her mid-teens. Instead, she lived until she was in her mid-forties. Her parents never put her into a care home but chose to take care of her in their own home her entire life. It was a very selfless act. After their daughter passed away they still had their health and could have spent some retirement time doing things they had missed out on as caregivers. However, instead they continued to relive the loss of their daughter. They talked about nothing else and told the same stories over and over again. Eventually, their own health began to fail and they ended up in the care home. I couldn't help but think that because their past purpose had come to an end they no longer had a *raison d'être*. With no new vision for their own future, they merely rehearsed their past as life passed them by.

CURSING THE PAST

We encounter people every day who just cannot stop cursing whatever injustice it is they have suffered. *My mother didn't love me. My stupid boss passed me over for a promotion. My heartless wife left me for someone with more money.* There is always someone else to blame, of course. Trust me on this one—nobody likes to be around a whiner. In fact, it's a sure-fire way to lose whatever friends you do have.

> WHEN YOU FINALLY GET TO THE PLACE WHERE YOU HAVE STOPPED TALKING ABOUT IT, THEN YOU ARE PROBABLY FREE. IF IT CONTINUALLY MAKES ITS WAY INTO YOUR CONVERSATION, THEN YOU ARE NOT.

There is a simple test to discover if you have been healed of a past hurt. When you finally get to the place where you have stopped talking about it, then you are probably free. If it continually makes its way into your conversation, then you are not.

I have an acquaintance who lost his job under really unfair circumstances. He has not been able to find an equivalent career and has struggled financially as a result. This is going to sound insensitive, but when I see him coming I start thinking of ways to avoid him. Wherever the conversation starts, it always ends back at how he was unjustly dismissed and how maybe he should have sued and on and on. He curses his past every time I see him. And I give him the same advice every time, "Forget about it and move on." I am convinced that because he cannot let it go, he cannot move on. He has a little yellow rope tied around his leg, and until he learns to untie himself from the past he is stuck.

> *He that cannot forgive others, breaks the bridge over which he himself must pass if he would ever reach heaven; for everyone has need to be forgiven.*
>
> — George Herbert

Nursing the Past

The first thing out of Gideon's mouth was that he was the "least and the weakest." He was nursing his insecurities. Paradoxically, many people get their identity from their adversities or inadequacies, not their strengths and accomplishments. People with handicaps or illnesses often allow their sense of selfhood to become defined by what is wrong with them, not what is right. We all have things from our past that we could harbour in ways that prevent us from moving forward. It is tempting to carry our hurts like they are precious cargo.

A close friend of ours was diagnosed with breast cancer. She told us about it, wanting the prayer support, but she told almost no one else. I asked her why she had chosen to keep it a secret. She responded that it was not a matter of secrecy but of being unwilling to let her disease define who she was. Many times people with cancer suddenly become known as "cancer victims." Some people will speak to them in quiet, concerned tones while others want to know all the gory details. Almost every conversation begins with the requisite, "And how are you doing, sweetheart?" The illness not only defines them but their relationships.

Most people fall into this trap. Immersed in the medical machinations of their treatment, they want to share the details of their newly discovered insights. Though this is not wrong in itself, they often become consumed with themselves and their medical journey. They may talk endlessly about drugs, physiotherapy, the latest research, etc. My observation is that they stop asking how others are doing because they cannot see past their own infirmity. In many chronic cases of illness, individuals can actually become demanding and ornery. It is not that they are bad people; they have simply lost control of their lives and are battling to regain some sense of self-determination. Unfortunately, it has led them to become self-focused.

Our friend with breast cancer figured this out from observing how others dealt with it, and she was not willing to go there. She has been waging a successful battle against the disease, all the while relating to others just like she always did before. The handful of people who are privy to the struggle respect her approach and are letting her live her life like there is no impediment. This level of privacy may not be for everyone, but it was her way to avoid nursing the past in order to avoid getting stuck in it.

In 1971, eleven-year-old Roger Crawford was playing tennis against the backboard at the local tennis club. The club pro, Tony Fisher, noticed the lad, who had been there every day that week, struggling to hold his tennis racket. On this particular day, Fisher went over to say hello. He reached out to shake Roger's hand, only to realize that Roger didn't actually have any hands.[2]

When Roger emerged from the womb, his parents were startled by what they saw. The baby's arms and legs were shortened, and he had only three toes on his shrunken right foot and a withered left leg, which would later be amputated. There was a thumb-like projection extending directly out of his right forearm, and a thumb and one finger stuck out of his left forearm. He had no palms.

Roger was born with a rare birth defect called ectrodactylism. The doctor informed his parents that Roger would probably never walk or care for himself. The Crawfords decided right then and there that they were not going to let this proclamation determine what Roger could or could not do. They elected to raise their son in the exact way they would any other child. They would not let his disability define him and insisted that he would never be given preferential treatment.

> "My parents always taught me that I was only as handicapped as I wanted to be," said Roger. "They never allowed me to feel sorry for myself or take advantage of people because of my handicap. Once I got in trouble because my school papers were continually late," explained Roger, who had to hold his pencil with both "hands" to write slowly. "I asked Dad to write a note to my teachers, asking for a two-day extension on my assignments. Instead, Dad made me start writing my paper two days early!"[3]

Roger's father also encouraged him to get involved in sports. They spent many hours in the back yard, practicing catching the football. At age twelve, the one-legged Roger managed to win a spot on the school football team. Rather than focusing on his obvious handicaps, before every game Roger would visualize his dream of scoring a touchdown. Then one day he got his chance. The ball landed in his arms, and off he ran toward the goal line as fast as he could on his artificial leg, his coach and teammates cheering wildly.

At the 10-yard line, a guy from the other team caught up with Roger, grabbing his left ankle. Roger tried to pull his artificial leg free from the player's grasp but instead ended up pulling his leg clear off. Roger hopped across the goal line on one leg. Roger recalls the moment, saying, "The referee ran over and threw his hands up in the air. Touchdown! You know, even better than the six points was the look on the face of the other kid who was holding my artificial leg."[4]

Roger's love of sports continued to grow and so did his self-confidence. He approached every obstacle as just another opportunity. One day, Roger stumbled upon an odd-looking tennis racket in a sports shop and accidentally wedged his finger between its double-barreled handle. The snug fit made it possible for Roger to swing, serve and volley like an able-bodied tennis player.[5] He began practicing every day and that was when he met Tony Fisher. This was the beginning of a lifelong friendship, as Tony helped Roger achieve incredible success for any tennis player, let alone one with no hands and one leg.

WE HAVE A GOD WHO CAN TAKE ALL OF THE FAILURES AND MISTAKES WE HAVE MADE AND RENDER THEM VOID, SET OUR FEET BACK ON TRACK AND LEAD US INTO OUR GOD-GIVEN PURPOSE.

Roger completed his high school tennis career with a win record of forty-seven wins and only six losses. He went on to play for the Loyola Marymount University in Los Angeles. He also became the first and only athlete with four impaired limbs to compete in a National Collegiate Athletic Association (NCAA) Division 1 college sport and to be certified by the United States Professional Tennis Association as a tennis professional. Today, Roger Crawford is an in-demand, award-winning inspirational speaker. He discourages audiences from being negative and from listening to the naysayers in their lives:

> The only difference between you and me is that you can see my handicap, but I can't see yours. We *all* have them. When people ask me how I've been able to overcome my physical handicaps, I tell them that I haven't overcome anything. I've simply learned what I can't do—such as play the piano or eat with chopsticks—but more importantly, I've learned what I *can* do. Then I do it with all my heart and soul.[6]

We can change the past. While I have serious doubts that we will ever find Steven Hawking's "worm hole in the space/time continuum" to enable us to travel back in time, it does not matter, for I am convinced that we have something far better. We have a God who can take all of the failures and mistakes we have made and render them void, set our feet back on track and lead us into our God-given purpose.

Chapter Seven

Lift Up Your Eyes

If you don't know where you are going, any road will take you there.

— Lewis Carroll

ONE OF THE most interesting expressions in Scripture is "lift up your eyes." It appears again and again in various narratives and always has to do with God's leading. Abraham and Lot had a squabble in Genesis 13 about whose livestock were whose. They decided to go their separate ways. Abraham gave Lot first choice, allowing him to pick the well-watered plain by the Jordan River. Abe wasn't sure what to do and God said, *"Lift your eyes now and look from the place where you are—northward, southward, eastward, and westward; for all the land which you see I give to you and your descendants forever"* (Genesis 13:14–15). His destiny was right in front of him; he just needed to lift up his eyes and see it.

When Jacob was labouring away under the hardship of his uncle Laban, God said, *"Lift your eyes now and see, all the rams which leap on the flocks are streaked, speckled, and gray-spotted; for I have seen all that Laban is doing to you"* (Genesis 31:12). Jacob could have run away and started over, but instead he lifted up his eyes and saw an opportunity. He asked to be paid with the inferior striped and spotted sheep, a request with which the shrewd Laban readily agreed. He then came up with a bizarre plan to place them behind striped fences, and, perhaps miraculously, many gave birth to striped and spotted sheep. Jacob was able to prosper with what he had, right where he was. He discovered the power of lifting up one's eyes.

In John 4:35, Jesus said to the disciples, *"Do you not say, 'There are still four months and then comes the harvest'? Behold, I say to you, lift up your eyes and look at the fields, for they are already white for harvest!"* Once again, their destiny was right in front of them. They just needed to lift up their eyes and see it.

IF YOU ARE LOOKING BACK, YOU CANNOT GO FORWARD.

As mentioned in the introduction, if this book was based on just one Bible text, it would have to be Philippians chapter three. I have preached from it dozens of times, but more importantly, I live by it every day. I think it is more instructive on finding our place in God's great big space than perhaps any other text throughout Scripture.

> *Not that I have already attained, or am already perfected; but I press on, that I may lay hold of that for which Christ Jesus has also laid hold of me. Brethren, I do not count myself to have apprehended; but one thing I do, forgetting those things which are behind and reaching forward to those things which are ahead, I press toward the goal for the prize of the upward call of God in Christ Jesus.*
>
> PHILIPPIANS 3:12–14

One day during recess, the on-duty teacher was having a difficult time with four boys in the schoolyard. In order to settle them down, he proposed a race from one end of the field to the other. If it was an ordinary race, everybody knew who would win, so he came up with a novel approach. The winner would be the one who ran the straightest, not the fastest. He would judge them based on how straight their tracks were in the freshly fallen snow.

Each of the four boys chose a unique approach. The first one ran looking backward to see if his tracks were straight. The second ran looking at his feet to see if they were going straight. The third looked across to the other boys in an attempt to run straighter. The fourth boy looked at the goal line at the other end and ran straight for it. It is not hard to predict who the winner was. The boy who focused on the goal at the end ran the straightest.

As obvious as the conclusion to this story might be, it serves as a metaphor for how many people live their lives. Someone once made this astute observation:

> Defeat comes from looking back
> Discouragement comes from looking down
> Distraction comes from looking around
> Destiny comes from looking forward

DEFEAT COMES FROM LOOKING BACK

There is a reason why they put a great big front windshield on your car and a tiny little rear view mirror. What is in front of you is far more important than what lies behind.

How many people do you know who spend their earthly existence looking back at the past? It could be the hurts or it could be the victories—it doesn't really matter. If you are looking back, you cannot go forward. We have to decide if we are going to spend the rest of our lives as victims or not. If you are still not clear on this, reread chapters two and three. It is a sign of old age when you begin to repeat yourself. It is a sign of old age when you begin to repeat yourself.

"...one thing I do, forgetting the things which are behind..."
PHILIPPIANS 3:13b, *emphasis added*

DISCOURAGEMENT COMES FROM LOOKING DOWN

When Abraham was seventy-five years old and childless, God told him to look at the stars in the sky and then He said, *"So shall your descendants be"* (Genesis 15:5b). For a barren couple of advanced years to be told something like that would be a cruel joke—that is, if it weren't true. God did not want Abraham looking down at where he was but looking forward to the possibilities that only God himself could produce. Twenty-five years later, God delivered the impossible and Abraham had a son who would become the very first in the line of the Jewish people. *"And not being weak in faith, he did not consider his own body, already dead (since he was about a hundred years old), and the deadness of Sarah's womb"* (Romans 4:19).

Abraham had to lift his eyes up from looking down at his problem to see the promise that God had in store for him. It took twenty-five years, but eventually he got it. How long we wallow in our own misery is probably up to us. Some of us are so negative that if we were put in a darkroom we would develop.

WE NEED TO LOOK FOR THE PROMISE INSTEAD OF THE PROBLEM. IN DOING SO, WE TURN THE OBSTACLES INTO OPPORTUNITIES.

Nothing is quite as discouraging as looking down at your current troubles and not seeing any clear way out. A sense of hopelessness quickly sets in, and you feel you have absolutely nowhere to go. The apostle Paul gives the proper perspective on this "head down" posture:

For our light affliction, which is but for a moment, is working for us a far more exceeding and eternal weight of glory, while we do not look at the things which are seen, but at the things which are not seen. For the things which are seen are temporary, but the things which are not seen are eternal.

2 CORINTHIANS 4:17–18

The struggles of this life are considered only a temporary light affliction. This is coming from the guy who wrote most of his epistles while he was in prison, waiting to be beheaded. Today when preachers come to town, they will often ask what kind of hotel we are putting them up in. Do you suppose Paul wrote ahead and asked, "What's your jail like?"

Nevertheless, the secret is not to look at the present circumstances, for they are temporary, but to look at the unseen answer that lies ahead. We need to look for the promise instead of the problem. In doing so, we turn the obstacles into opportunities. Yes, I know how cliché that sounds. I also know it is the absolute truth and one of the keys to getting us through in life.

One day a few years ago, I went to the hospital to visit my brother who was recovering from a broken neck (I tell this rather sad story in chapter fifteen). He was hospitalized for weeks, and he had a new roommate almost every week. As I walked into the room, he asked me if I had meet Osman. I introduced myself to the young Eritrean man, who was wearing a cast from his ankle to his hip. His leg was elevated in front of him in such a way that he spent all day looking at his injured limb.

"What happened to you?" I asked. In a rather discouraged tone, he told me that he was standing at bus stop on his way to work when a car drove up the curb and ran him over and busted up his knee.

"Whoa, that is nasty!" I responded. "What did it do to your knee? Was it your ACL, your PCL, your MCL or your LCL?" I asked, as I pointed out the various locations of those ligaments, followed by the ridiculous statement, "I'm a knee expert, you know."

Somewhat excited, he responded, "I don't know what it did!"

"Well, we could find out. We just need to get the nurse to check your chart. I could find out for you before I leave," I assured him. By the time I had completed my visit with my brother, I had forgotten about my promise to Osman. "Well, it was nice meeting you," I said as I walked by his bed.

"I thought you were going to check my chart," he replied anxiously.

"Oh, sure . . . I guess I could do that," I offered, as no nurse had come by the entire time. Making my way to the nurses' station, I asked if they had the chart for Osman in Room 512, bed one.

"Sure," said the nurse, and without even looking up she handed me the chart. As I held the medical chart in my hand, I realized that maybe I wasn't really a knee expert, seeing as I could barely make sense of anything I was reading. It was all written in medical terms—who would have thought? Then I spotted a word I recognized: 'patella,' the kneecap.

Speaking to the nurse, I said, "It looks like he broke his patella and they wired it back together."

Again without looking up, she said, "Yup, that's what they did."

Returning to the room, I said, "Osman, I have good news for you. Your ligaments are fine; you just broke your kneecap." I grabbed his good knee and gave the patella a couple of little swirls. "They had to wire the thing together and you should be as good as new in no time," I reassured him.

Then with big, moist, puppy dog eyes, he asked if he would ever play soccer again. "Well, Osman," I confessed, "you need to understand I'm not a real doctor, I just play one on TV. But I don't see any reason why you won't play soccer again."

At that moment my brother, who had been listening this whole time, reacted, "Oh, please! You have no idea what you are talking about."

"What do you mean? I am just trying to bring Osman a little hope. What's the crime in that?" I defended.

"What's the crime? You're impersonating a doctor!" my brother insisted. "I am pretty sure that IS against the law."

I assured him that my mission in life was to bring a little ray of sunshine into the lives of others, and again I bid the two of them *adieu*. A couple of months later, both out of the hospital, my brother ran into Osman. He was back playing soccer.

When we look down at a problem or predicament, we become fixated on it and find it very hard to move on. But there is another aspect of *looking down* that we often don't think about. Sometimes we are not in a bad place while we are looking down but in a good one. Your present situation may be one of victory or accomplishment and you may want to live there for the rest of your life. Forgive me for saying it, but that is not going to happen. Although, I did have a friend who loved high school so much, he repeated Grade 12 three times! Even to this day, he talks about those years as his glory days. For every mountaintop experience, there are at least two valleys—the one you crossed just before it and the one on the other side of the summit.

In the story of the Mount of Transfiguration, Jesus took John, James and Peter to the top of a mountain. There they experienced an incredible, but somewhat indescribable, transfiguration of Jesus and Moses and Elijah. Peter got all excited like he usually did (the only time his mouth was empty was when he was changing feet) and said, *"Lord, it is good for us to be here; if You wish, let us make here three tabernacles: one for You, one for Moses, and one for Elijah"* (Matthew

91

17:4). Peter desired to remain there in that moment of his mountaintop experience forever. Jesus let them enjoy the moment, but then they went back down the mountain and re-engaged in life.

> *My expectations are sky low, because I'm standing on a mountaintop.*
>
> — Jarod Kintz[1]

I had just boarded a plane and was heading west for my speaking tour in Saskatchewan. I squeezed myself into one of the plane's seats, which seemed narrower than the last time I flew, and I began to pray, "Oh Lord, please don't let me have some jumbo-sized person as a seat mate today." I was not being mean, just selfish. I had work to do and did not have the energy to fight with a Japanese sumo wrestler for the armrest. As a man the size of a VW Beetle waddled right by, I said beneath my breath, "Thank you, Jesus." A tiny young Chinese lady came on the plane and I said, "Yes, Lord!" But it was not to be. Then an almost inhumanly gigantic creature of mythical proportions stopped at my row and said, "I think I am with you." He folded his massive sinewy athletic frame into the aisle seat and his five-foot broad shoulders displaced my entire torso, pressing my bewildered face up against the window as I gasped just to breathe. From my now tiny corner of the universe, I began reading a boat magazine. My new seat mate asked me if I had a boat.

I said, "Yes, a speed boat," and asked him the same question. He told me he preferred human powered boats.

"You mean kayaks or canoes?" I responded.

"Something like that," he said.

Something like that, indeed! To make a long story short, I was sitting beside Adam Kreek, the gold medalist for eight-man rowing in the 2008 Beijing Olympics.

Adam is now a motivational speaker and he crosses the country sharing the story of his team's victory for Canada in Beijing. It was not an easy journey. After winning the world championship in 2003, they went into the 2004 Athens Olympics favoured to win the gold. They came in fifth. They continued to train six days a week, and in 2007, they won the world championships again. Favoured to win the Olympics in 2008, this time they made no mistake and won the gold by half a boat length. It was a great story, and I loved hearing it firsthand from the very person who had lived it. Adam had his slide presentation open on his laptop and I noticed a page titled Gold Medal Syndrome, so I asked him about it. He told me that GMS was the belief that you will be a different person after you win the medal than you were before. When Olympians discover that a gold medal has not made them into a different person, they often go into a depression. He said that winning the gold medal was the greatest four hours of his life.

"Then what happened?" I asked.

"After that," he said, "nobody knew who I was."

I then mentioned that it would probably come as a huge surprise, but that I had never actually won an Olympic gold medal myself and I wanted to know how Gold Medal Syndrome would relate to me. He explained that it doesn't matter what we do in life, we are not different people after our accomplishments and we had better find our identity somewhere else. It is a great message for all of us to keep in mind. The true measure of a person is who they are inside, not what they do or achieve on the outside. I really enjoyed my visit with Adam Kreek. Here was a young guy with his head really screwed on right. He knew a lot about victory, and defeat (not to mention a great deal about team work), and consequently, he knew a lot about life.

At the conclusion of our flight, he asked me if I had ever held an Olympic torch. I told him I had left mine at home. To my surprise, he pulled an Olympic torch out of the luggage rack overhead. His Beijing team was given the honour of carrying the torch on the first leg of the Vancouver 2010 Olympic Torch Relay. Because he was the one sharing the story, they gave the torch to him as a keepsake. I am quite certain that holding that torch is as close as I will ever get to being an Olympian, but for a few moments I got to touch the glory.

As it turns out, that's all anyone gets—just a few moments of glory.

DISTRACTION COMES FROM LOOKING AROUND

Mankind has never before lived in a time of such immense distractions. If you live in an urban centre, you will be accosted by 5,000 advertisements in a single day. They will be everywhere you look—billboards, the bus stop bench, the bus itself, the gas pump, the elevator, the bathroom stall—you don't get a moment of peace. While you are watching the football game, the entire field somehow turns into a giant Coke bottle. Your computer and smartphone are even worse, because Google, Facebook and other big-brother-esque corporations have been monitoring your web browsing. They can target their advertisements to your interests, down to the exact make and model of the item for which you might be looking. It's a bit frightening, actually. Then there is the time-wasting YouTube, endless online shopping . . . and, oh . . . there are even things we can do for fun *offline*, if you can find time. It is a wonder we can get anything productive done at all with these distractions around us. People often ask me how many people actually work at Church of the Rock. I usually say, "About half of them."

Medical journals are now reporting that the occurrence of ADHD (attention deficit hyperactivity disorder) has increased 42% among young people in the last ten years.[2] What is that all about? Is it something in the water? Our food? Perhaps, but maybe it is more sociological than neurological or psychological. Since we have already established that I have no trouble impersonating a doctor, my professional take is that we may be distracting our kids into it. They are more inundated with images than any generation before them. They are the first generation almost completely raised on computers and video games.

I was having a discussion about some internet thing with my son, who is a computer engineer. When he told me the technological answer, which seemed very obscure, I asked him how he knew that. He said, "Pop, I'm *from* the internet." My son thinks he is *from* the internet. Apparently, I did not explain the facts of life to him correctly.

The developing brains of young people have been bombarded with tens of thousands of killings in movies and video games and entertained by more brain wave stimulating music videos than were even possible a decade ago—they have been trained through technology to have the attention span of a gnat. Whether I am correct about this or not is less important than the fact that we are the most distracted people in human history.

One of the lowest days in King David's life started when he allowed himself to be distracted.

> *It happened in the spring of the year, at the time when kings go out to battle, that David sent Joab and his servants with him, and all Israel; and they destroyed the people of Ammon and besieged Rabbah. But David remained at Jerusalem.*

2 SAMUEL 11:1

It was the time of year when kings were supposed to go to war, but David stayed home in Jerusalem. David had lost his focus; he had taken his eyes off the prize and perhaps had become bored with it all.

With his men all out fighting for country and honour, David remained in his Hugh Hefner silk pajamas and stared blankly out the window. What did he see? The beautiful Bathsheba bathing on her rooftop. I don't want to spend much time describing the scene, lest I fall into the same trap as David, but suffice it to say that, even back then, I am sure women bathed naked. David called for her and slept with her.

A few weeks later Bathsheba discovered herself pregnant with the king's child. David, still unwilling to come clean, sent for her husband Uriah, who was still off at war with the king's army, hoping that he might sleep with her so they could pass the child off as his own. Uriah, being a more honourable and focused man than David, refused to sleep with his wife while his fellow soldiers were entrenched in battle. David escalated his despicableness and had Uriah sent to the front lines of battle, where he was killed. Then David quietly took Bathsheba as his own wife, thinking he had avoided the consequence of sin. But the prophet Nathan called David on his behaviour, and a week after birth, the child died. Every sin has a consequence.

There is much we can learn from the story of David and Bathsheba, but for my purposes the lesson is just how far off track distraction can lead us. Not only does it cause us to stray from our goals and purposes, but it can destroy our virtue and character as well. David was distracted by another man's wife. Although few of us would admit it, most of us are guilty of being distracted by what others around us have too. We get caught up in the swirl of peer pressure so easily. It is true with regard to material things, like having the right car, house, TV or lawn mower.

But far worse than merely being distracted by material things, we also begin to take on the values of the world around us. We get caught up in the competitiveness of the workplace, striving for that promotion without regard for what we really want to do with our life.

Maybe we even get the promotion we chased, only to find ourselves with less time for our families. Countless folks pursue the "American dream" instead of determining their priorities and purpose first. I have old friends who are so consumed with living in the "right" neighbourhood, joining the "right" golf club and sending their kids to the "right" schools, that they have no unique purpose for their existence except to keep up with the Joneses. I always tell them, "Even if you win the rat race, you're still a rat."

LOOKING AHEAD

... but one thing I do, forgetting those things which are behind and <u>reaching forward to those things which are ahead</u> ...

PHILIPPIANS 3:13, *emphasis added*

The Smith Corona typewriter company was established in 1886. They invented the first typewriter that could type in both upper and lower case. By the early 20th century, they owned the typewriter market and were buying up their competitors' products and companies and staying well ahead of the curve.[3] It was not until 1933 that a company by the name of International Business Machines (IBM) entered the flourishing typewriter business. Along with several other companies like Remington, they duked it out for market share as the post-war demand for typewriters took off.

Then, in 1951, the computer was invented. IBM saw the future, and by 1953 had produced their first version of it. Never mind that it took up the space of an entire room and had the computing power of your garage door opener—the world had changed forever. Smith Corona kept plugging along, building typewriters as IBM investigated the fledgling arena of computers. By 1995, Smith Corona had declared bankruptcy. IBM, on the other hand, has annual revenues year after year in the $72 billion range.[4] One company looked down at where they were, while the other looked forward to where they were going.

The boy on the school yard who kept his eyes on the prize was the clear winner in the end. Regardless of where you have been, where you are now or where others are going, focus on where you are *going*. The goal posts that we erect for our lives are the very things that will determine our future. Successful people are always goal setters; they begin with the end in mind. People who look only at the finish line always finish first.

Chapter Eight

You Can't Steer a Parked Car

You've got to be very careful if you don't know where you're going, because you might not get there.

— Yogi Berra

WHEN I WAS maybe seven years old, we were just about to leave church after a typically boring service. My mother had loaded all of us kids into the car and we were finally going home when she realized that she had forgotten her coat in the church. She told us to "sit tight" and she would be right back. For whatever reason, she left the keys in the ignition with the engine running. I climbed over the seat from the back and sat in the driver's seat. Swinging the wheel back and forth, I declared, "Look, I'm driving!" My smart aleck six-year-old brother, Tod, immediately told me that I wasn't and that the car wasn't moving. He said I needed to pull the lever down.

I pointed to the gearshift and said, "This one?"

"Yup, that's the one," he calmly remarked.

"Should I pull it?" I asked.

"I would." He smugly responded.

Acting on his bad advice, I pulled it right down and off we went. The car moved slowly at first since it was idling. I could not reach the pedals, but it didn't matter anyway since I would not have known what to do with them.

"I'm driving!" I exclaimed in delight. At first I was doing reasonably well, trying to steer around the other parked cars, but there were just so many of them. And like all good things, my joy ride came to an end—in the side of Mr. Mackenzie's brand new Pontiac.

I was too young to comprehend how my father must have settled the score with our neighbour, but I do remember how mad he was at me. In fact, he was so mad that he never let me drive the car again until I was sixteen. Nevertheless, I learned a very important life lesson at an early age: you can't steer a parked car.

Knowing exactly where you are going in life sounds great, but what if you just don't know? Do you just wait? Do you just exist, hoping that someday you will be hit by lightning and know exactly what to do?

Firstly, I know people who have been hit by lightning, and it is not a good thing. One childhood friend of mine has been struck or nearly struck three times and has lived to tell about it. To be honest, it has made her a little paranoid to go outside. Although one time, she got hit sitting in her living room watching TV—she walked away unharmed, but the television was fried and she missed the entire episode of her favourite soap opera. Such a tragedy!

BUT WHAT IF YOU JUST DON'T KNOW? DO YOU JUST WAIT? DO YOU JUST EXIST, HOPING THAT SOMEDAY YOU WILL BE HIT BY LIGHTNING AND KNOW EXACTLY WHAT TO DO?

Most of us will not get a divine declaration from above as to what to do with our life. Even Abraham, to whom God spoke directly, had no clue where he was going when he departed from the Ur of Chaldeans for the Promised Land. *"By faith Abraham obeyed when he was called to go out to the place which he would receive as an inheritance. And he went out, not knowing where he was going"* (Hebrews 11:8). Knowing only he was going somewhere, he pulled up stakes (literally) and hit the road. Abraham and his family dwelled in tents their entire lives. God led him as he went on his way.

The exact same thing happened with Moses and the children of Israel when they tried to return to the Promised Land after 430 years in Egypt. They did not know where they were going either. God led them by a pillar of fire by night and a cloud of smoke by day. The Bible is clear that the purpose of the fire was to illuminate their path. It did not run way ahead of them. In fact, when they stopped moving, the fire and cloud stopped as well.

You cannot steer a parked car. More often than not, God will direct us only after we have made a decision and are moving forward.

> *"A man's heart plans his way, But the Lord directs his steps."*
> PROVERBS 16:9

People often ask me if I visualized a church of thousands of people—with ministry all over the world and broadcasting a nationwide television program—when we started the church in 1987. I would love to say that I had a vision for all of this and it has come to pass just as I planned, but nothing could be further from the truth. In 1987, I had a vision to try to reach 100 people in attendance. I had a vision to try to get through another week with enough money left over to pay the pastor (me) a salary. I just kept moving forward, extending the vision a little bit every month or year. When I look back, I still marvel at how far we have come. The key, I believe, is to just keep moving forward and let God direct (or redirect) your steps along the way.

I remember reading an article in the *Economist* years ago that said the three steps to success are:

1. Finish high school
2. Get married and stay married
3. Never leave a job until you have another job lined up

The article never promised that this model would make you as successful as Bill Gates but only that in general you will do just fine. In today's world, you would probably need to update the first point to "finish high school and university." The principle, however, is to simply keep moving forward.

The cycle of quitting and starting over again and again ultimately leads to failure. When we quit something, we often have to start the whole process again. In times past, most people would settle into a career and stay there. If they were halfway competent, they would become very good at what they did, be promoted through the ranks, receive pay raises and likely retire early with a full pension.

My father-in-law, Bob, started working in construction, building grain elevators in Saskatchewan in his early twenties. He rose through the ranks to become a foreman, then a project supervisor, and eventually he joined management. At sixty-one, he retired with a fully indexed pension. As of this writing, he is ninety-seven years old and has lived comfortably on his pension for almost as long as he worked for it in the first place. As a side note, he is still in good health and drives his own car every day. He might be one of the oldest drivers on the road and hasn't had an accident in fifty years.

Today, the average person has seven different careers. Not different jobs—different careers! I understand that people want to find something that is fulfilling and meaningful to do with their life, but a short attention span will doom them to continually beginning again. I know many people my age who are still trying to figure out what they should be doing for a career when they should really be thinking about a post-career endeavour of pursuing a passion, which may ultimately be a volunteer role.

When we keep moving forward in the same direction, we more often than not become very good at what we do and, consequently, very successful. If you look around the world at the biggest churches, for instance, they have one thing in common: a pastor who has been at it a very long time. For many years, the largest church in North America was First Baptist in Dallas, Texas. During that time, the pastor was W. A. Criswell. He pastored the church for fifty-one years, well into his eighties.[1] The largest church in Winnipeg used to be Calvary Temple, and Rev. H. H. Barber was there forty-four years, also into his eighties.

GET RICH SLOW

One of the most common questions I get asked is, "Pastor Mark, how do you preach week after week for forty-five minutes without relying on notes? Is it because you are brilliant?"

I usually jokingly respond, "No, it's because I'm illiterate, and can't read them." Well, the real reason I can't read my notes is because I should be wearing glasses when I preach, but I am far too vain to let glasses disrupt my Hollywood good looks.

But to answer the question more seriously: when you do something (anything) long enough, as I have been saying, you get good at it! It is really that simple. I've been preaching every week for more than thirty years. I'm bound to get better at it sooner or later. If people would hunker down and commit to doing a career for the long haul, they would get very good at it and eventually they would do it almost effortlessly. Why do professional jugglers never drop the balls and make it look so easy? Because they have been doing it a long time and are now good at it.

Unfortunately, our society sells instant gratification. This is why people buy lottery tickets, go to Vegas or lose their shirts on some harebrained Ponzi scheme. Everybody is looking for the "get rich quick" plan. It doesn't exist. But the "get rich slow" approach does!

Having said all this, life is not about getting rich or becoming successful; it is about discovering our destinies and allowing God to lead us into His purposes.

LIFE IS NOT ABOUT GETTING RICH OR BECOMING SUCCESSFUL; IT IS ABOUT DISCOVERING OUR DESTINIES AND ALLOWING GOD TO LEAD US INTO HIS PURPOSES.

Charles Paul Conn, the president of Lee University in Cleveland, Tennessee, wrote about an interesting encounter in his book *Making it Happen*. Some years before when he was living in Atlanta, Georgia, he was going through the Yellow Pages of a phone book and looking for a restaurant. One in particular caught his attention. It was called the *Church of God Grill*. This peculiar name aroused his curiosity, so Conn dialed the number for the restaurant. A man answered with a cheery, "Hello! Church of God Grill!" Conn asked the man how his restaurant had been given such an unusual name. The owner gladly shared the story, saying, "Well, we had a little mission down here, and we started selling chicken dinners after church on Sunday to help pay the bills. People liked the chicken, and we did such a good business, that eventually we cut back on the church stuff. After a while, we just closed down the church altogether and kept on serving chicken dinners. We kept the name we started with, and that's 'Church of God Grill.'"[2]

I have read this story several times in other books, mostly in a critical fashion. The writers will make the point of how sad it is for a church to lose their vision for ministry. I wouldn't disagree with that part of the story, but I think they ignore the other side of it. Maybe this pastor was better at frying chicken than he was at preaching the gospel. If he wasn't effective in ministry because it wasn't actually his calling, then he should have done what he was called to do. I don't see any shame in running a restaurant if that is where your gifts and passions lie. I don't want to be closed to the possibility that Pastor Grilled Chicken planned to serve the gospel but his calling was serving fried chicken. *"A man's heart plans his way, But the Lord directs his steps"* (Proverbs 16:9).

> Why did Colonel Sanders cross the road? He heard there was chicken on the other side!

You may have your own "chicken story" of when your direction in life took only a slight turn and yet it seemed like everything changed. As I mentioned earlier, I have never had the luxury of a clear, compelling direction from God. He has just gently nudged me along the way.

In 1996, Church of the Rock did not have a building and we were renting space from Trinity Television in Winnipeg. The principals of that ministry were our good friends, Willard and Betty Thiessen, who were the hosts of the daily television program *It's a New Day*. They had a nice sized conference room that we rented for our church services on Sunday mornings. In those days, the church numbered around 200 people, counting children, adults and pregnant women (twice). Willard and Betty were in the planning stages of trying to launch a 24-hour Christian television station. It was an ambitious endeavour.

Every once in a while I get very graphic dreams that seem to contain divine direction. One night, I had a convoluted dream about a traffic light and television ministry. It is a bit hard to explain, but in the dream I saw a blinking yellow light. I also knew somehow that it was directly related to television ministry. When I awoke, I lay in bed trying to figure it out and it came to me. I decided that green would have meant "go" and red would have meant "stop," so blinking yellow must mean "proceed with caution." I figured that God must have given me a message for Willard and his 24-hour station. After all, he was the only person I knew in television ministry. I called him up, told him I had something to share with him and offered to buy him lunch. During our meal, I shared the dream with a fair bit of enthusiasm, only to be met with polite indifference. While driving back to the office I was almost annoyed that it wasn't met with excitement, when it was as if I heard God say to me, "Who said the dream was for Willard?"

"Well, if it wasn't for him, then who was it for?" I thought. Then it suddenly dawned on me that the dream was for me. We were meeting in a television studio, there were cameras in the next room and one of my good friends was an independent television producer. My destiny was right in front of me but I just wasn't seeing it. Like Abraham and Jacob and many others, I needed to lift up my eyes and see it.

My next meeting with Willard was to re-interpret the dream as being for me and to ask him what he thought about it. He showed enthusiasm this time and offered to rent us the equipment on Sundays to tape our program. I then visited the small MTN network that broadcast into our city from an hour away in Portage la Prairie. Almost to my surprise, they loved the idea and gave us their most preferential airtime rate.

Within just weeks, we found ourselves in the television ministry. It was a remarkable feat for a small church of our size, but nothing is impossible with God. I still knew that I needed to be obedient and proceed with caution, so we made a decision that we would never allow television ministry to consume us as a church. We would only buy airtime with cash and never on credit. We would only expand as there were funds to do so, and we would never ask the viewers for money. If this was going to be a God endeavour, then He would have to supply. It was ten years before the program began to air coast to coast. It was a relatively slow journey, waiting for the doors to open and God to direct our steps. In all these years we have never asked for money or bought airtime on credit.

If God leads, he also provides. Chances are your destiny is right in front of you, but you cannot steer a parked car.

Chapter Nine

No Goals, No Glory

If you aim at nothing you will hit it every time.

— Zig Ziglar

I DON'T WANT anyone to get the idea from the previous chapter that goals are not important. They are immensely powerful. When we set real goals (ones we actually plan on pursuing), we will almost always achieve them.

I press toward the goal for the prize of the upward call of God in Christ Jesus.

PHILIPPIANS 3:14, *emphasis added*

In 1966, Lou Holtz was a twenty-eight-year-old unemployed football coach. He came to the conclusion that if he just let life happen he was never going to get anywhere. He sat down and wrote out a list of lifetime goals. This was no ordinary list. Most things on it were of a grand nature—for example, becoming head coach of Notre Dame Fighting Irish, winning a National University football championship, landing a plane on an aircraft carrier, eating dinner at the White House, and meeting the Pope. Eventually the list grew to 107 bold, mostly lofty, goals. As of this writing, he is still alive today and is still pursuing his dreams. Of the 107 goals, he has accomplished 95 of them, including all the ones I already mentioned. Now retired from football, he is a motivational speaker who is fond of saying,

Write down everything you hope to achieve in life. . . .
Then make sure you do something every day to realize one
of your dreams. You are going to encounter adversity . . .
but you will also find yourself waking up hungry to take
big, satisfying bites out of life. [1]

One of the things you will hear from Lou Holtz in his speeches,
is that if you're bored with life—you don't get up every morning with
a burning desire to do things—you don't have enough goals. The
prophet Habakkuk said almost the same thing:

Then the Lord answered me and said:

"Write the vision
And make it plain on tablets,
That he may run who reads it.
For the vision is yet for an appointed time;
But at the end it will speak, and it will not lie.
Though it tarries, wait for it;
Because it will surely come,
It will not tarry."

HABBAKUK 2:2–3

Because goal-setting works, we should set goals. Set goals for
your finances, business, fitness, weight loss, sports accomplishments
. . . everything! Write them down, just like Mr Holtz said. And just
like Mr. Habakkuk says, he who reads them will run with them. Who
will read them? You will! And you will see most of them come to pass.

GOALS PROVIDE US WITH MOTIVATION

Although goal-setting is an immensely powerful tool, it is not
something magical or supernatural in and of itself. However, it does
focus our entire existence toward the accomplishment of our goals.

Vince Lombardi, the legendary coach of the Green Bay Packers, once quipped, "If winning isn't everything, why do they keep score?"[2] Whether it is in sports or in life, goals provide us motivation.

When our kids were younger we put them in mini-soccer. Sure, they called it soccer, but I called it "pack ball." The entire pack of kids would all chase along behind the ball. The ball would pop out once in a while and they would all chase it in a new direction. As a coach-type parent, I would be yelling at my five-year-old to break for the open space and wait for the cross from midfield. She would stop momentarily to put her hands on her hips and glare at me in disgust as if to say, "Dad, do you know absolutely nothing about this sport?" before she would rejoin the pack in chasing the ball. If that wasn't frustrating enough for a competitive father, the fact that they did not keep score drove me even crazier.

On the very first game of the year, I arrived late. I anxiously turned to a fellow parent and asked the obvious question: "What's the score?"

She responded, "This is mini-soccer; they don't keep score."

"They don't keep score? Then how do you know who is winning?" I asked incredulously.

"You don't. That is the whole point. We don't want any of the kids to feel like losers," she instructed me condescendingly.

What kind of Eastern mysticism sport did I get my daughter into? If nobody wins, then they're all losers, I was thinking to myself. So, being the uber-competitive soccer dad, I took it upon myself to call out the score from the sidelines.

"It's three to two for the red team!" I shouted out. They didn't even have team names, just colours. Not only did I get disapproving looks from the other parents (mostly the mothers), but I got bawled out by the fifteen-year-old coach at the end of the game. Apparently, I didn't understand fair play and sportsmanship.

*Whoever said, "It's not whether you win or lose that counts,"
probably lost.*

—Martina Navratilova[3]

The fact is, goals are important. No professional sporting event in the world could exist if they did not keep score. However, the goals that are truly important are not the ones you score but the ones you set. Countless people bump along through life with no sense of goal. In the absence of goal-setting, we live according to the "tyranny of the urgent." We must act or we will be acted upon. Otherwise, someone or something else will determine your path in life, and they won't have your best interests in mind. Nobody should ever be satisfied with that scenario.

WE MUST ACT OR WE WILL BE ACTED UPON.
OTHERWISE, SOMEONE OR SOMETHING ELSE WILL
DETERMINE YOUR PATH IN LIFE, AND THEY WON'T
HAVE YOUR BEST INTERESTS IN MIND.

In 1952, David Pryor of Camden, Arkansas, fell in love with the political life of Washington DC and secured a summer job as a congressional page. He was smitten by the place and decided right then and there that he would one day return as the elected representative for his home state of Arkansas. When no one was looking, he carefully hid a dime behind one of the many statues and vowed that one day he would return and retrieve it. In 1966, a full fifteen years later he arrived in Washington as the newly elected congressman for the state of Arkansas. He approached the press gallery, held up the penny that had been hidden for all those years and told them the story. Then he said, "This should teach us two things: number one, never underestimate the dreams of youth, and number two, they don't clean this place very often."[4]

GOAL-SETTING POINTS US IN THE RIGHT DIRECTION

Someone once said the best way to get a bullseye is to shoot an arrow at a wall and then draw a circle around it. Goal-setting is important, if for no other reason than it points us the right direction. The Bible has more to say about goal-setting than most people realize. Proverbs 29:18a says, *"Where there is no vision, the people perish"* (KJV). Other versions use the phrase "the people cast off restraint." Those who live without vision and goals live without the guideposts that keep us moving in the right direction.

One of the funniest sports stories of all time happened during the 1929 Rose Bowl. The Georgia Tech Yellow Jackets defeated the California Golden Bears by a score of 8–7. Doesn't sound like much of a game! But it is how they won that made it go down in sports history. Georgia Tech fumbled the ball and Roy Riegels of the Golden Bears scooped it up and headed for the goal line, making it down to the one yard line. His celebration was cut short when he discovered that he had run the ball back the wrong way. It was fellow Golden Bears player Benny Lom who was named player of the game for his attempt to tackle his teammate Riegels before he scored on his own team. The two-point safety on the next play proved to be the margin of victory for Georgia.[5] It is like Yogi Berra said, "If you don't know where you're going, you'll wind up somewhere else."[6] We laugh at how ridiculous this story is until we realize that, in our own way, we have all done the same thing. We have all run toward the wrong goal line in life.

I could continue to talk about the power of goal-setting and how we can accomplish everything we have in our hearts to do, and it would all be true. But as I said in the introduction, there have been thousands of books written on the subject of human potential and positive thinking. I am more interested in helping people *find their place in God's great big space*. Whatever goals we set we are likely to achieve, and therefore, it is essential to set the right goals. We can have all kinds of selfish, materialistic or meaningless goals, and because of the power of vision, we will likely see them come to fruition. But what is the point of accomplishing goals if they are the wrong ones?

A friend of mine named Vin has a story to which most of us can relate. He always had a bit of a love affair with the Ford Mustang. He set a goal that one day he would own one. When the 2006 model came out with the retro look, he knew he "needed" that car. As a Safeway grocery store employee, a brand new Mustang was probably out of the question. However, Safeway was having an employee incentive contest and the winner got 2,000 Safeway stock worth $25,000, or a Mazda Miata. Vin ended up winning the contest. He could not believe his good fortune. The chance to fulfill his dream had come. He didn't think twice about taking the stocks, as a Miata ain't no Mustang. He promptly sold the stock and headed down to the dealership.

Vin and his wife, Rose, had determined they would be satisfied with a practical V6 version of the pony car. That day, however, they drove off the lot with a brand new Mustang GT model with a V8 and every other possible option. It was a dream come true, that is, until the first snowfall, when the wide-tired, rear wheel drive muscle car got stuck in two inches of snow. Vin still loved the car anyway and drove it for a few more years until he admitted just how impractical it was for their use. He sold it and bought a front wheel drive Ford Tempo. Apparently, any sense of automobile snobbery had been purged out of him.

There is an addendum to the story. Had he held onto the Safeway stock for just a few years, Vin could have bought a fleet of Mustangs. The stock split when it reached $32.00 per share, which would have given him 4,000 shares. Then after a few years, it split again at about $52.00, which would have put him at 8,000 shares. By the time he sold the Mustang, if he had kept all the shares, they would have been worth $208,000. Vin is a great guy with a super positive attitude so he doesn't live with regrets, but he does ask himself the question once in a while if maybe, just maybe, the Mustang wasn't the right goal. Nah!

GOAL-SETTING IS A GOD-GIVEN PRINCIPLE THAT PROMPTS US TO PURSUE WHATEVER IS IN OUR HEART.

We probably all have a Mustang story. The old expression goes something like this, "You had better be careful for what you wish for," because you will probably get it. The stronger the desire we have to achieve something, the more likely it is to come to pass. I believe goal-setting is actually a God-given principle that prompts us to pursue whatever is in our heart (Proverbs 29:18). Goals can, however, become so easily misdirected toward things, money, pleasure, world domination or whatever!

I don't want to rain on anyone's "bucket list," but our goals need to reflect the higher aspirations of life. If you accomplish a litany of self-indulgent fantasies during your lifetime but have failed to enrich your world along the way, I guarantee you will find yourself feeling empty at the end of your days. Listen to the words of King Solomon at the end of his life. He speaks like a person who is profoundly empty in heart. He was one of history's most accomplished men, and yet he concludes,

I made my works great, I built myself houses, and planted myself vineyards. I made myself gardens and orchards, and I planted all kinds of fruit trees in them. I made myself water pools from which to water the growing trees of the grove. I acquired male and female servants, and had servants born in my house. Yes, I had greater possessions of herds and flocks than all who were in Jerusalem before me. I also gathered for myself silver and gold and the special treasures of kings and of the provinces. I acquired male and female singers, the delights of the sons of men, and musical instruments of all kinds.

So I became great and excelled more than all who were before me in Jerusalem. Also my wisdom remained with me.

Whatever my eyes desired I did not keep from them.
I did not withhold my heart from any pleasure,
For my heart rejoiced in all my labor;
And this was my reward from all my labor.
Then I looked on all the works that my hands had done
And on the labor in which I had toiled;
And indeed all was vanity and grasping for the wind.
There was no profit under the sun.

ECCLESIASTES 2:4–11

In 2007, Rob Reiner produced the movie called *The Bucket List*. It was the story of two terminally ill seniors (Jack Nicholson and Morgan Freeman) who wanted to fulfill a list of things they always wanted to do before they die or "kick the bucket."[7] I am not sure if Reiner coined the term "bucket list" or merely popularized it, but it has become part of our vernacular. You hear people today talking about their own bucket list and the things they want to accomplish in life. They usually want to climb Everest or skydive or scuba dive or some other kind of dive before they die.

I need to confess that I have always had a bucket list of sorts. Mine mostly have to do with seeing the world. The Holy Land was near the top of the list. I was less concerned with seeing it before I died and more concerned with getting there before someone blew it up. As it was, we got there just after the last war with Lebanon, and the tourists were nowhere to be found. The Great Pyramids of Giza were another must-do for me. We visited them for our twenty-fifth wedding anniversary. Having accomplished these goals, I am no less convinced of the veracity of goal-setting, but I have started to rethink the value of the things on my list.

Each summer since I was a kid, we have taken our summer vacation on Lake of the Woods in Ontario. Since then, my recreational therapy has always been to run around the lake in a powerboat, exploring the thousands of islands and bays. I always told people that one day I would like to run the entire length of the eighty-mile lake from the north side (where we are) to the south side, where the city of Warroad, Minnesota, is located. It is not exactly a Marco Polo accomplishment, but it was still something that I wanted to do. The distance is certainly not insurmountable; the challenge is getting a day when the weather allows you to cross Big Traverse Bay. This one stretch of water is forty miles long by forty miles wide, without any islands. When the wind comes up, the waves can swell to seven or eight feet high, making it impassable to virtually any typical runabout lake boat.

I have a friend who pastors a church in Warroad, and he invited me to come and preach at his church one summer. How good was this? Go preach the gospel, and at the same time, check a major lifelong goal off the list. I barely slept the night before as I ran the details of the trip over and over in my head: extra gas, warm clothes, drinking water, and of course, a cell phone in case we had mechanical problems and ended up stranded in the middle of Big Traverse. As it turned out, there was no cell phone reception, so it was good thing we didn't break down. I had carefully plotted the route on my GPS, since Lake of the Woods is a treacherous waterway with countless rocks and reefs, and once you're into Big Traverse you cannot see land for quite some time.

Kathy and I set out at 7:00 AM, and we set a rapid pace of a steady 40+ MPH in order to get there before the service started at 10:00 AM. At the halfway mark, we had to go through customs at a remote US border phone booth at what is called the Northwest Angle, a cartographical mistake that has left a chunk of the USA in Canada. Apparently we have Ben Franklin to blame for the blunder. We reached the station just after 8:00 AM, so things were looking good. The US customs phone booth is pretty much out in the bush and runs basically on the honour system. The uncommonly cheerful customs lady answered the phone on the first ring. We gave her our names, passport numbers and boat registration numbers. She then wanted to know, of course, if we were carrying any citrus fruit—as if to say, "You can transport all the guns and drugs you like, just don't bring us any dang fruit." One definition of a Canadian is "an unarmed American with healthcare."

Cleared for entry, we made our way to the opening of Big Traverse Bay and came around the corner of the last island blocking our way to a straight shot to Warroad. This was the moment I had waited my whole life to see. As the wide expanse of water stretched out in front of us, we were met with wall after wall of three- to four-foot waves. Even as we slowed our pace, the waves crashed over the bow. Less than a mile out, we were forced to retreat and abandon our journey. It was over as soon as it had begun.

Almost comically, we now we had to re-enter Canada. I had called Canada Border Services the day before to ask about the location of their remote border crossing phone. A most unhelpful agent told me it was on the east side of Cyclone Island. I informed her that it was a large island surrounded by rocks and that I needed to get the location correct. I told her that Google Earth showed that side of the island as uninhabited and that perhaps it was on the west side. She responded with a (no joke) "Whatever!" Turns out I was right, it was on the west side. It had a brand new $100,000 dock. The phone booth however, was out of order. The sign said, "If phone is not operational, call [this number] on your cell phone." This seemed reasonable, except THERE WAS NO CELL SERVICE THERE IN THE MIDDLE OF NOWHERE!

Eventually we found a summer resident on another island with a phone. I needed to call the pastor of the church as well, since he was standing on the dock in Warroad waiting to pick us up. This day was not working out well for anyone. I made it up to my friend and preached at his church two weeks later. However, this time we went by car to ensure that I did not leave him hanging a second time. Turned out it was a perfectly calm day and we would have made it by boat in half the time it took by car.

What about my dream of crossing the Big Traverse? I now don't care if it ever happens. "But Pastor Mark, you can't let your dream die," you might say. Why not? I have decided it is not important. I now feel like it was a misguided goal. In the greater scheme of things, what does it matter? It was just a self-indulgent desire. The fact that I was on my way to preach was merely a justification.

There is nothing intrinsically wrong with our bucket list dreams, but if they serve no greater purpose than bragging rights then they really are not that important. If I swore to myself that someday I would jump out of a plane and then one day I did, how would that change anything? Would it make my world a better place? Would it even make me a better person? Well it might, if I had some irrational fear I was trying to overcome, like the irrational fear of falling to one's death at terminal velocity from 10,000 feet above the ground.

Don't get me wrong, I am not against life goals that are of purely a dream-fulfilling nature. They often make us stronger and more resolute people. What I am saying is that we cannot live our lives for the sake of a list. We need to live for a purpose, a purpose greater than ourselves and our personal accomplishments. At the end of our lives, it won't matter how many planes you jumped out of, how many bridges you jumped off, or how many Big Traverse Bays you traversed. What will matter is how you touched the lives of others, how you made your world a better place and how many people you brought with you into heaven. That is why I needed to return to Warroad and preach the gospel, but it didn't matter if I went by boat or not. Maybe I will have another crack at Big Traverse, maybe I won't. I won't be a lesser person if I don't.[†]

The CBC's *Fifth Estate* did a very fascinating story called "Into the Death Zone."[8] It dealt with the fad-like desire for non-mountaineers to climb Mount Everest. Because it is not a particularly technical climb, it is within the grasp of many people who are in excellent physical condition and have the $50,000 or more to pay a tour company. The program followed the story of a Nepalese-born Canadian woman by the name of Shriya Shah-Klorfine. Somewhat un-athletic and completely inexperienced, she was determined to check Everest off her bucket list. May 19, 2012, was a particularly deadly day on Everest when the mountain claimed four lives. Shriya's was one of them. She had been told many times during the climb to turn back, but she would not. In the painfully slow nineteen-hour ascent she had used up all her oxygen. Her obsession to reach the top compelled her to press on, even though she was out of oxygen and

---

[†] Incidentally, in the *The Bucket List*, our heroes died without fulfilling their lists.

physical strength. Through incredible mental strength and determination, she succeeded in reaching the summit and her goal, only to be unable to make the return climb in the pitch darkness of night. Ultimately, her guides abandoned her and she was left to die. It is a very sad and disturbing story on many levels. It seems like such a waste of a life in exchange for a few brief moments of personal satisfaction.

There is another Canadian/Everest story with a much better ending. During the 2006 climbing season on Everest, Calgary schoolteacher Andrew Brash and his team were challenging the summit. An experienced climber who had bested many of North America's toughest peaks, Brash was well trained and prepared for the ultimate prize of Everest.

They began their final ascent at 9 PM on May 25, and climbed through the night. Only 200 metres shy of the summit, they came across a grisly discovery. Australian climber Lincoln Hall was lying on the side of the path, clinging to life. Suffering from extreme altitude sickness, his own team had abandoned him and left him for dead. He had lain there alone for twelve hours, and his wife and teenage daughter had already been informed by satellite phone of his death. Brash called off his own team's ascent of the summit to try to rescue the dying Hall. They spent many hours in the -25°C temperature assisting his recovery and planning a way to get him back down the mountain. Finally, with the help of a Sherpa rescue team, they were able to return him to base camp where he walked the last stretch on his own. Other than losing the tips of his fingers and a toe to severe frostbite, Lincoln Hall made a full recovery.

This story stands in stark contrast to another that happened during the same climbing season. English climber David Sharp died in a similar situation in the "death zone" (the area within 600M of the summit) of extreme exhaustion. It was reported that over forty climbers passed right by—and sometimes over—the suffering Sharp on their way to conquering the summit.

Upon returning to Calgary, Andrew Brash was surprised to discover that he became more famous for saving a life on Everest than for reaching the summit (he returned to Everest almost two years later to the date in 2008 and conquered the peak). He was welcomed with much fanfare and become somewhat of a hero to the students at the school where he taught. When asked by reporters if it was a tough decision to give up a shot at the summit, Brash will reply that at the time he didn't realize he was doing anything out of the ordinary—that it just seemed like the right thing to do.[9] Although I have never met Brash, he is a hero to me as well. He understands what has true value; the life of another human being should always trump a personal achievement.

Again, I am not saying we should not set personal goals, but if we want to find our place in God's great big space, we need to raise our goals to a higher level. We need to start envisioning things that will somehow touch our world and give glory to God.

Chapter Ten

So, Who Do You Be?

It's not who I am underneath, but what I "do" that defines me.
— Bruce Wayne (*Batman Begins*)[1]

KATHY AND I both graduated from the same high school, just not at the same time (since I am four years older than her, which she will remind anyone who will listen). So when our school celebrated its fiftieth Anniversary reunion, we both had a reason to attend.

And no, I did not graduate fifty years ago! But I have a lot of good memories and I really loved high school. As I like to joke, it was the best five years of my life. I could have stayed there forever. In fact, thanks to Mr. Albertson, my chemistry teacher, I almost did. I just could not figure out those chemical equations. Either he was a poor teacher or I was not paying attention. Or maybe I was just plain stupid—but I just didn't get it and I went to at least half the classes. Nevertheless, somehow I graduated, which meant eventually I would make an appearance at the high school reunion.

It is remarkable how many actually stay away from their reunions. I guess they are just happy to have the painful, awkward years from ages fifteen to thirty-five behind them. Reunions produce a moment of truth of sorts—did you live up to your yearbook quip? Mine was, "Most likely to ask: Would you like fries with your order?"

Our reunion was a great event; it is good to see people that you have not seen for decades, especially if you look better than they do—slimmer, more hair, that sort of thing. But inevitably, the question still gets asked: "So, what are you doing now?" The reason we ask is only partly because we are genuinely interested. The other underlying motivation is that we measure and value people by what they "do"! If they have a prestigious career or make a lot of money, we immediately have a higher opinion of them. If they do something very common, we are less impressed. "Are you really a rocket scientist, Bill? WOW! And, you're a stay-at-home mom, Jill? Oh, good for you." Turning back to Bill, "So, tell me, Bill, what's it like, working at NASA?"

It was fascinating to see how many different career paths my old classmates followed. Some were engineers, doctors, insurance salesmen, real estate, policemen and contractors. Only a few showed up who were in the unenviable position of being unemployed or underemployed. There were a couple of people who had become wildly successful. These were the ones everybody was talking about.

"Did you see Raymond and Lil? They showed up in a chauffeur-driven limo!"

They were hard not to notice with their Mazatlán tans and their hair and breast implants (not on the same bodies). Raymond struck it rich when the company he worked for had a gold mine hit pay dirt. Prior to this, being cash poor, they were paying him in company shares. When they discovered gold, his shares became worth a gazillion dollars. It was hard for everybody not to be impressed.

We have a perverse love affair with the rich and famous. That's why those supermarket magazines like *People*, *Us*, and *Star Weekly* sell so well.

Then there was Bob. What about Bob? He was getting a lot less attention. He might have been the only currently unemployed person to be brave enough to show up at the reunion. He had just lost his job as a tampon sales representative. We used to call him "Mr. T." I am not making this stuff up! He was very popular with his wife's friends, as he always had lots of boxes of sample tampons that they were free to take home after a visit. Where does a tampon salesman go to revive his career when he is almost in his mid-fifties? On the other hand, Bob is tremendously talented with his hands. He has restored antique boats, motors, toys and all kinds of other things. He drives a mint condition, fully restored, peach and cream-coloured 1955 Nash.

When I looked at the clear financial dichotomy between these two classmates who both graduated near the middle of their class, it got me thinking. Is Raymond's life of more value than Bob's? Does his economic stature make him any smarter, better or more significant? One of the greatest tragedies throughout history has been the cruelty and indifference with which we have treated our fellow human beings. It has always been a function of the fact that we think there are people who have less value than others. I think we have got it all wrong.

It is an almost inescapable reality that we value people by their economic success over just about anything else. Personally, I think this is a terrible barometer. Some of the biggest jerks I know are also the richest people I know, and some of the poorest people I know are the kindest and most generous. There is nothing about wealth that can possibly make us better humans. The kind of people we are comes from within, and it is impossible to measure that from our accumulations or accomplishments.

If we are really honest, we have all valued ourselves on some sort of material level at one time or another. Often it is on the basis of a possession. If you have ever bought a brand new car, you know what I am talking about. You drive it off the lot with such pride in your heart that your nostrils are flaring. You imagine that every other driver on the road is looking at you with envy, wishing that they, too, had your car—because I am sure they have never seen a Toyota Corolla quite like yours before.

To be perfectly truthful, I have never owned a new car, but I did have a pretty snazzy boat, so I know the feeling. When I would drive up to the dock in my 250 horsepower outboard speedboat, there was only one way to put it—it was awesome! I bought the boat out of Florida, and it was completely trashed by the sun and salt water. It took ten months to restore it. I had so much unhealthy personal pride wrapped up in it that I had to let it go. I sold the boat to an acquaintance, who emailed me after his first day on the water. Guess what words he used? "It was AWESOME!" I could almost hear his nostrils flaring. Maybe for you it has never been a car or boat but a giant TV or a motorcycle or a really great pair of shoes (if you are female) . . . or something. We are all guilty at some level.

Recently, Kathy and I visited Marco Island in Florida. It is a very unique place on the southwest tip of the state and was once a mosquito-infested mangrove island. Today, it is a beautiful city with expensive homes and condos on gorgeous beaches. The streets are lined with flowering hedges and palm trees, and the grass is manicured to within an inch of its life. It is as pristine a city as I have seen anywhere in the world. There is virtually no crime, graffiti or littered back lanes. The people are so ridiculously friendly, you feel like you might be on the set of *The Truman Show*. "Good morning, and in case I don't see ya, good afternoon, good evening, and good night!"[2] I am always interested in the history of a place, and so, we made a visit to the island's historical museum.

The story of the island is fascinating, but I want to focus on only one segment of it. In 1962, the Mackle brothers, Elliott, Robert and Frank Jr., purchased most of the island for $7 million and began transforming it. They cut ninety-seven miles of canals so that most residents could have waterfront property. They had a vision—not to make money but to build a one-of-a-kind island city. They donated the land for schools, parks, churches and museums. The project proved immensely popular, and thousands bought into the "Florida dream." The Mackle brothers would sell off new lots in order to develop more of the island. Each step of the project required government approval to dig more canals.

By the 1970s, the environmental movement had risen up in Florida and the development ground to a halt. People began to realize there was important ecological value to the mangroves and Everglades that used to be considered marshy wastelands. The Mackle brothers were now in a predicament, since many of their presold lots could no longer be developed. They could have declared bankruptcy and left the new investors holding the bag, but instead they sold off almost all of their assets in order to return the money to these purchasers or swap them for land that could be developed. In the end, the Mackle brothers lost most of their wealth and were almost completely broke, but at great personal cost the dream survived. They put their principles and integrity above their own financial survival. Purpose trumped economic success. They lost their shirts but were true to themselves and never lost sight of their character and their vision.[3]

OUR TRUE PURPOSE IN LIFE TYPICALLY COMES OUT OF "WHO" WE ARE, NOT "WHAT" WE DO. WHO WE ARE ENDURES LONG PAST WHAT WE DO.

Here is what you need to know about finding our true purpose in life. It typically comes out of "who" we are, not "what" we do. Who we are endures long past what we do. It is "who" we are which propels us to keep doing "what" we do. The "what" in and of itself has little sustaining power. It will eventually become tedious and boring without an underlying greater purpose born out of our character, vision and motivation, which is "who" we are.

After Moses died, having failed to lead the children of Israel into the Promised Land, Joshua took charge of the herd. He had a formidable task, and to be honest, a far more clear purpose than most of us get for our lives. As Joshua was about to lead the great nation of people across the Jordan River, God spoke to him very clearly:

> No man shall be able to stand before you all the days of your life; as I was with Moses, so I will be with you. I will not leave you nor forsake you. Be strong and of good courage, for to this people you shall divide as an inheritance the land which I swore to their fathers to give them. Only be strong and very courageous, that you may observe to do according to all the law which Moses My servant commanded you; do not turn from it to the right hand or to the left, that you may prosper wherever you go. . . . Have I not commanded you? Be strong and of good courage; do not be afraid, nor be dismayed, for the Lord your God is with you wherever you go.
>
> JOSHUA 1:5–9, *emphasis added*

Three times, God tells Joshua who he should BE (strong and courageous) while at the same time observing what he was asked to DO. It seems God was more interested in who Joshua was as man than what he was called to do. Simply put, the "who" we are determines the "how" and "why" of "what" we do. Sorry, I couldn't resist. If you reread it, it will actually make sense.

When men, in particular, greet each other for the first time, the second question out of our mouths after "What is your name?" is "So, what do you DO?" We measure people by what they do instead of who they are. We know that God had given Joshua a very clear "what," but that doesn't seem to be nearly as important as the character behind the task. The question, therefore, should not be, "So what do you DO?" but "So, who do you BE?" Maybe this is not the best grammar, but it more accurately describes what really determines our true worth and value.

THE QUESTION, THEREFORE, SHOULD NOT BE, "WHAT DO YOU DO?" BUT "WHO DO YOU BE?"

About twenty years ago, I met another young pastor at a conference. We both had small upstart churches. In the course of the conversation he began to talk about how he wanted to be on television. In those days, televangelists had a terrible reputation, and I have to admit that I had my own subtle contempt for them. When I asked him why he wanted to be on TV, he told me because he thought he would "look really good" on television. It was one of the stupidest reasons I had ever heard. I understand comments like that from Kim Kardashian, but from a minister of the gospel? I am sure you see the irony in this, since I am the one with a weekly television show seen across the nation, and as far as I know, he is still muddling along. Maybe he's visiting the doctors for hair implants and plastic surgery to keep up his amazing looks. I don't know.

It is so easy to miss the mark when it comes to what is really important. We live in a world that seems to be obsessed with the rich and famous, the likes of Donald Trump and Paris Hilton. I am too—but because I love to make fun of them. Imagine, all the money in the world, and yet, the poor Donald can't get a decent haircut.

I have my own heroes. Few of them ever made any money, but they all changed their world. They were all people who figured out that who you BE is more important than what you DO. They are people like Mother Teresa of Calcutta, who gave her life for the poorest of poor in India; C. T. Studd, who gave his for the people of China; and Dr. David Livingstone, who spent his entire productive life bringing the gospel and modern medicine to the people of Central Africa.

At our core, we will always act or DO based on who we are, or BE. God's command to Joshua was all about who he needed to BE, which in his case meant *strong and courageous.* After all, he was about to lead a civilian company into a hostile land and conquer it. In many ways, we live in a hostile land. North Americans are not militarily hostile, but we are constantly swimming upstream concerning our values and morals. The cultural pressure to BE and DO in conformance to those around us is far more intense than most of us realize. We do not have to go to Africa or India to start to BE before we DO. We simply have to determine who we want to BE, regardless of what we do. If we are in business, are we going to BE honest? If we are employees, are we going to BE hard working? If we have position and power, are we going to BE humble? You get the picture.

We are a sporting family. Kathy and I were both athletes in our own right and raised our children to be involved in competitive sports. Though perhaps not for every family, we felt sports was a great arena for our kids to develop character and virtue. Oh, we trained them to win, all right, but we also taught them that who they were on the playing field was far more important than what they accomplished. Unless you are Tiger Woods or Michael Jordan when it comes to sports, you are going to lose more often than you win. We influenced our children to be good losers as well as gracious winners. We told them that, at the end of the day, inner strength was far more important than outer strength.

When our daughter was in high school, their basketball team managed to eke out a place in the Provincial championships. They were far from the best team and were going to get soundly tromped somewhere along the line. The girls rallied and managed to earn a place in the quarter finals. They were buoyed by their success, and their newfound confidence brought their game up to a whole new level. Facing one of the better teams, it was back and forth for the entire game, and right up to the last minute it looked like they might pull it off. In the end, they lost by two points and then (for me), the real entertainment began.

I've learned something about women over the years. They seem to cry when they are happy and they cry when they are sad. Well, I am pretty sure these girls were sad because they became inconsolable. The team members were sobbing and sobbing and embracing each other. Meanwhile, my daughter had a big smile on her face. She had played the game of her life and just did not see anything worth crying about. Having competed in dozens of different sports and having won and lost her fair share, this was just another day at the office. As they went down the line of players shaking hands, she was the only girl smiling and genuinely congratulating the other players.

As she was coming off the court, one of the mothers intercepted her and said, "Danica, what is the matter with you? Do you have no remorse at all?"

Remaining calm, and not dismissive at all, she responded, "Well, unlike some others, I don't get my identity from whether I win or lose." I could not have been more proud of my daughter. She truly understood what we had been trying to instill in her for all those years. She drew on her inner strength—she had demonstrated who she BE. "Who" you BE determines "what" you DO!

After graduating from high school, our daughter was the only student in the history of her school to ever earn a place on a university sports team. Not only did she make the team, she won a full four-year scholarship and in her rookie year was the starting setter for her university's women's volleyball team. It was a great honour and an even greater opportunity. She would compete at a far higher level than she had ever in the past and travel the nation. It was very exciting that, at such a young age, she would see the cities and universities of Canada.

The experience, however, was much different than we had anticipated. Elite sports can often be a harsh place for a young girl. One of her coaches, as much as I appreciate her as a person, employed the old-school coaching techniques of negative motivation and criticism. This, unfortunately, cast a very heavy pall over the entire team. The girls began to snipe at each other and cast blame for a bad play or a lost game. Needless to say, they did not have a good year on a number of different levels. The bigger challenge for our daughter was that she found herself travelling every weekend with a group of girls that do what college girls sometimes do. If they won a game, they might head out to a bar and overdrink. If they lost a game, they would do pretty much the same thing. Instead of seeing the sights of the cities, they were seeing the insides of the nightclubs. The pressure to go with the flow was ever-present. Our daughter found herself mostly standing alone as one who would not head to the bar on their many out of town trips. Although they respected her for it, it did not go a long way in building camaraderie. No one really likes a party pooper. She had to draw again and again on her inner strength.

On the other hand, she was a tremendously positive influence on them. She was always smiling, joking and offering sensible advice when others found themselves in a predicament. By the end of the season however, she realized that this was not what she signed up for. She missed spending time with her family and friends, as well as life outside of volleyball. I remember the day she sadly decided she was not going to return the next year and was going to let the scholarship go. As parents, we struggled along with her in the decision as well.

She said, "Pop, you don't know what it is like to live every day in a hostile environment!" Well, I do actually; I work in a church! (That was a joke, in case you missed it.) In the end, she had to be true to who she was. What she did—playing volleyball—was not nearly as important as who she was. We need to BE before we DO!

Chapter Eleven

The Greater Purpose

What we do for ourselves dies with us. What we do for others and the world remains and is immortal.

— Albert Pike

I press toward the goal for the prize <u>of the upward call</u> of God in Christ Jesus.

PHILIPPIANS 3:14, *emphasis added*

WHILE I WAS writing this book, I met a man named Don, who was just retiring. He had led an interesting life that had taken him into several business adventures. He owned a cheque-cashing business as well as one that had something to do with games of chance tear-off tickets, or as he appropriately dubbed them, "rip-off tickets." None of these endeavours were what he had intended to do with his life, but as I mentioned in an earlier chapter, our lives almost always get steered in new directions as we go on our way. It seemed as though he had been very successful and had done well financially.

When I told him I was writing a book, he wanted to know what it was about. I told him it was about finding one's purpose in life. Without hesitation, he told me he wanted a signed copy because he was still trying to find his purpose. He was not joking, and in fact, he was very sincere. He was sixty-seven years old and still searching, even though he had retired from a very lucrative career. He told me he was not satisfied with what he had done with his life and wished it had been more meaningful. I appreciated his honesty.

Don was expressing what I have seen again and again in ministering to people. Everybody wants their life to count for something. They all want to know what their purpose is. That is why Rick Warren's book *The Purpose Driven Life*[1] has become the bestselling non-fiction hardcover book in history, selling 33 million copies. Not the bestselling *Christian* book—the bestselling of *any* non-fiction book.[2] Making money, although it pays the bills, is not very fulfilling. Placed deep within the heart of man is a desire to make a difference in the world.

To get back to the question from the introduction, why are we here? The oversimplified answer is: for God's good pleasure. We exist for the same reason our children exist. We deliberately bring them into this world as an extension of ourselves. The pattern should not be lost on us. If you wanted to start a family, what is the first thing you would do? You would establish an abode. Buy a house or get an apartment. Decorate the nursery—blue for a boy, pink for a girl. That's what God did, except fortunately he used a full palette of colours. He created all these things first and then put Adam in the centre and said, "*It is good.*" Everything that exists was created so He could provide us somewhere to live. It seems like overkill, but only if you don't understand that He is a BIG GOD.

So God built a BIG abode because He is a BIG God who apparently wanted a BIG family.

> *And God said to them, "Be fruitful and multiply, fill the earth and subdue it."*
>
> GENESIS 1:28

This is the one thing we seem to be really good at. I sometimes think God created sex to trick us into having children. Seriously, would there be as many people in the world if . . . ? I don't think so!

This idea of family is not merely a metaphor. The Bible uses some very specific language when it comes to family. What is God called? God the *Father*. Jesus is called Jesus the *Son*. What are you and I called? The *children* of God . . . *brothers and sisters*. Family! God has thrust us all together as a family and caused us to relate to one another as we relate to Him. That is why He says, *"Love the Lord your God with all your heart, with all your soul, with all your strength, and with all your mind,' and, '[love] your neighbor as yourself'"* (Luke 10:27). It is all about relationship. This is not the deist view of God, where God stands back and watches the world unfold, uninvolved and indifferent. God created us so He could fellowship with us. Adam walked with God *"in the cool of the day"* (Genesis 3:8). Moses spoke to God *"face to face, as a man speaks to his friend"* (Exodus 33:11).

> *But if we walk in the light as He is in the light, we have fellowship with one another, and the blood of Jesus Christ His Son cleanses us from all sin.*
>
> 1 JOHN 1:7

Though we are to have fellowship with one another, the above verse is really talking about having fellowship with God. It's talking about personal relationship. To put this into perspective, how would you feel if you brought children into the world and received nothing back but pain and suffering? You cook for them, clean for them, drive for them, pay for them and they go about their lives like you don't exist.

> "Yeah, that just about describes it!" One exasperated mother with a teenager exclaims, "For this I got stretch marks?"

What do we want from our children more than anything else? We want relationship with them, no matter how old they are.

My wife, Kathy, had a real life encounter with this scenario. She used to work for Lifeline, a response system for elderly people who have an emergency button hanging around their necks. If they fall down, they push the button and say, "I've fallen down and can't get up." One day she got a call from a woman, ninety years old, who had gone totally blind. She just suddenly lost her sight and wasn't going to regain it. They got her down to the hospital but now something would have to change—they couldn't just send her home. Kathy tracked down her next-of-kin in another city.

She phoned these now middle-aged children and said, "Your mother has gone blind, and we need to know what you would like to do with her."

Her own children said, "She's not our responsibility!" We are appalled that someone would treat his or her own parent with such contempt. Yet we do that every day with God. People ignore Him, curse Him, deny that He even exists or feel that He doesn't have any significance to their lives. How is that any different from the heartless grown children of this poor blind woman? God created us for fellowship. He wants us to relate to each other, but He wants even more for us to relate to Him. The meaning of life is not quite that simple, but it does give us a context for the *greater purpose*.

> *Behold, children are a heritage from the Lord,*
> *The fruit of the womb is a reward.*
>
> PSALM 127:3

We have an innate desire to reproduce because we were created in the image of God. We are designed to participate in His procreative nature. I have seen many married couples who have found themselves infertile. It is heartbreaking to see them have to wrestle through this painful inevitability. It feels like something is profoundly missing in their lives. It is a bit hard to explain why, but it is not hard to imagine. That desire comes from the father heart of God. There is an unspeakable joy that comes from having children. It is a ridiculous amount of work. Kids are a huge responsibility, an immense expense and often the cause of great heartache. Yet, even when we have our bad days or even bad years, most of us would do it again in a minute. A woman with four sons who all ended up as criminals and spent much of their time in jail was asked if she would still have children if she had it all to do over again. She answered, "Sure, just different ones."

I realize that I tend to oversimplify everything, but I really see the greater purpose of God as this: God, like any parent, gets great joy from watching us interact with our world, each other and, ultimately, Him. The same reason we want to have children and enjoy seeing them grow up and engage their world is the same reason God created man. He is willing to put up with bad behaviour and heartache because of His great love for us.

The big objections that people have regarding a Creator are often more philosophical than scientific. People wrestle with the paradox of why God, if He is good, would allow evil in His world. They question why an all knowing God would put man in a place of temptation (Garden of Eden), knowing full well that he would fall and then be condemned to hell for doing so. These are not unreasonable questions to ask. What is unreasonable is to jump to the conclusion that therefore "there is no God," or that if there is, He is a malevolent monster and who would want any part of Him?

Could God have created a world free from evil and mankind free from the possibility of sin? Sure, but then there would be an aspect of humanity missing, the one thing that makes us human in the first place—free choice! The freedom to choose is what sets us apart, even from the rest of the animal kingdom. Most animals merely act on the power of instinct. That in itself is miraculous. If you have ever seen a cat give birth to kittens, it is remarkable. The mother cat instinctively knows to chew off the umbilical cord, clean off the kittens with her tongue and get down to the business of feeding them. I am trying to imagine my wife, Kathy, doing any of this with the birth of our children, but the mental image is somewhat frightening.

Humans need to be taught almost everything. Then they are confronted with tens of thousands of decisions during their lifetime, each one an opportunity to exercise their God-given freedom of choice. If God had created Adam and Eve without the temptation of the Tree of the Knowledge of Good and Evil in the midst of the garden, they would not really have had free choice. They would have served God because they had no other option and, I would argue, would not have been able to love God. Love is not a feeling but a choice. Without that choice, they could have robotically obeyed God but not truly loved Him in the proper definition of the word.

When we have children of our own, we want them to love us just as we love them, but we can't make them. They have got to make that decision for themselves and, fortunately, most do. That does not mean they will not give us moments of grief along the way—they will, lots of them.

God also longs for children that will love Him in the way that He first loved them. He is well aware that we will behave badly at times and that some of us will reject Him completely, but I would argue that it is a chance He is willing to take because the pay back is worth it: children who truly love Him and serve Him and make every effort to love His other children.

For the creation was subjected to futility, not willingly, but because of Him who subjected it in hope; because the creation itself also will be delivered from the bondage of corruption into the glorious liberty of the children of God.

ROMANS 8:20–21

God subjected His creation to futility—the potential for evil and corruption—in the hope that mankind would overcome the temptation and emerge as the children of God. Make no mistake about it, God has deliberately allowed us to live in a hostile environment. Call it a test if you will, but He is looking for people who will rise above the depravity of this world and choose to live for Him.

When Adam and Eve fell, all creation was thrust into a state of despair. You do not have to be a scientist to observe the unrest of the planet—earthquakes, typhoons, droughts, plagues, pestilence. We spend much of our energy fighting off the ravages of Mother Nature. She is not always a happy camper and she lets you know about it. If is not a drought, it is a flood. If it is not a hurricane, it is an earthquake. If it is not extreme heat, it is extreme cold. As Canadians, we have had some of our coldest winters ever in a decade of "global warming" . . . hmmm. No part of creation seems to be exempt from her wrath. It doesn't matter where you live. Creation itself is waiting for the children of God to become . . . well, the children of God.

For the earnest expectation of the creation eagerly waits for the revealing of the sons of God.

ROMANS 8:19

In the fullest sense, we will never be completed until Jesus returns, but in the interim we are meant to be transformed into the image of God. His greatest desire would be that his children would look like Him (figuratively speaking).

But we all, with unveiled face, beholding as in a mirror the glory of the Lord, are being transformed into the same image from glory to glory, just as by the Spirit of the Lord.

2 CORINTHIANS 3:18

There is a certain joy you get when you have a child that looks like you or your spouse. Kathy and I have three kids. Jordan, the eldest, looks so much like me that people will comment on how he is the spitting image of me when I was his age. Kristen, our second child, looks so much like Kathy that they have been mistaken as twins. No joke. For some strange reason, no one ever thinks Jordan and I are twins. Not sure why. Danica, our last child, ended up with a unique blend of both our features. Or as she likes to put it, "I got all of your good characteristics and none of your bad ones." She does not struggle with self-esteem.

It is not an accident that the New Testament uses the metaphor of family to describe everything about God and His people. He is the Father, Jesus is the Son and we are referred to again and again as brothers and sisters. If there is one message that the New Testament continually repeats, it is that God wants us to love Him by loving others.

"You shall love the Lord your God with all your heart, with all your soul, with all your strength, and with all your mind," and "your neighbor as yourself."

LUKE 10:27

"For I was hungry and you gave Me food; I was thirsty and you gave Me drink; I was a stranger and you took Me in; I was naked and you clothed Me; I was sick and you visited Me; I was in prison and you came to Me."

Then the righteous will answer Him, saying, "Lord, when did we see You hungry and feed You, or thirsty and give

You drink? When did we see You a stranger and take You in, or naked and clothe You? Or when did we see You sick, or in prison, and come to You?" And the King will answer and say to them, "Assuredly, I say to you, inasmuch as you did it to one of the least of these My brethren, you did it to Me."

MATTHEW 25:35–40

If someone says, "I love God," and hates his brother, he is a liar; for he who does not love his brother whom he has seen, how can he love God whom he has not seen? And this commandment we have from Him: that he who loves God must love his brother also.

1 JOHN 4:20–21

The greater purpose of life will almost always be played out in how we treat our fellow human beings. We can say we love and serve God, but it is evidenced primarily by how we love others. Perhaps if we would begin to see ourselves as siblings rather than neighbours in how we treat each other, we would take on a whole new perspective. Mother Teresa put it in an interesting way when she said, "The problem with the world is that we draw the circle of our family too small."[3] I think what we learn from people like Mother Teresa and Saint Francis of Assisi and Albert Schweitzer is that they figured out that why we are here has more to do with what we do for others than what we do for ourselves.

THE GREATER PURPOSE OF LIFE WILL ALMOST ALWAYS BE PLAYED OUT IN HOW WE TREAT OUR FELLOW HUMAN BEINGS.

Philip Yancey is one of my favourite authors. In his book *Where is God when it Hurts?* he comes to an interesting conclusion.

In my career as a journalist, I have interviewed diverse people. Looking back, I can roughly divide them into two types: stars and servants. The stars included NFL football greats, movie actors, music performers, famous authors, TV personalities, and the like. These are the people who dominate our magazines and our television programs. We fawn over them, pouring over the minutiae of their lives: the clothes they wear, the food they eat, the aerobic routines they follow, the people they love, the toothpaste they use.

Yet I must tell you that, in my limited experience, these "idols" are as miserable a group of people as I have ever met. Most have troubled or broken marriages. Nearly all are hopelessly dependent on psychotherapy. In a heavy irony, these larger-than-life heroes seemed tormented by an incurable self-doubt.

I also spent time with servants. People like Dr. Paul Brand, who worked for twenty years among the poorest of the poor, leprosy patients in rural India. Or health workers who left high-paying jobs to serve with Mendenhall Ministries in a backwater town of Mississippi. Or relief workers in Somalia, Sudan, Ethiopia, Bangladesh, or other such repositories of world-class human suffering. Or the Ph.D.'s scattered throughout the jungles of South America translating the Bible into obscure languages.

I was prepared to honour and admire these servants, to hold them up as inspiring examples. I was not, however, prepared to envy them. But as I now reflect on the two groups side-by-side, stars and servants, the servants clearly emerge as the favored ones, the graced ones. They work for low pay, long hours, and no applause, "wasting" their talents and skills among the poor and uneducated. But somehow in the process of living their lives they have found them. They have received the "peace that is not of this world."[4]

Mother Teresa of Calcutta once had a young woman write to her, asking if she could join the Missionaries of Charity so that she could make her life count as Mother Teresa had made hers count. She waited months for a reply. Finally, a hand written letter arrived with four words on it—"Find your own Calcutta."[5]

I don't think that means that we need to run off to Calcutta to find our purpose. Our destiny is right in front of us—we just need to lift up our eyes to see it. Whatever we are doing right now is a perfect starting point for making our life count for something bigger. All that is needed is a slight adjustment in motivation and then to start serving the people that God has already put in our path to love.

Our friend Carolyn found her Calcutta in Winnipeg's West End. Some twenty-five years ago she was employed at a large insurance company in our downtown area. When she worked late in the winter, it would already be dark by the time she headed for the parking lot. A kindly security guard named Douglas would often stay overtime to ensure Carolyn had safe passage to her vehicle. As a gesture of thanks, she made him a lemon meringue pie, which turned out to be his favourite.

That simple pie provided an invitation into Doug's very private world. He lived in a rooming house with nine other men on a rundown street in our city's West End. He was a war veteran, single, with so few worldly possessions he had not even a clock on the wall. He did his laundry in a five-gallon pail with a plunger. After Doug retired, Carolyn continued to visit him, as he struggled with respiratory disease and was unable to do simple things like lift himself into the claw foot tub at his home. The relationship grew and she cared for him like he was her own father. Carolyn introduced others to Doug and his roommates one Christmas by bringing by carollers and goodies. Together they began to hold birthday parties for him, would take him shopping, arranged for homecare and baths. Carolyn invited a lawyer friend from the church to come over and help Doug get his affairs in order. The love of God was never lost on Doug and he read and reread a little booklet that he had been given on the "sinner's prayer." After fifteen years of friendship, Doug finally said the prayer for the first time, inviting Christ into his life, all the while gripping the copy of the booklet in his now feeble hands. A year later, Doug died in Carolyn's arms.

If that was the end of the story it would still be a good one, but it is not. Carolyn had developed relationship with many of the residents in the rooming house and even the surrounding neighbourhood. She decided she was going to do something else for these others that she had grown to love as well. The owner of the rooming house, Mike, also owned a store in a nearby strip mall. In her irrepressible way, Carolyn asked him and the Hindu owner of the mall if she could borrow the parking lot do a Saturday afternoon "coffee break" for the community. Along with five other volunteers and their children, they served coffee and cookies that first year to the neighbourhood. Years later, the event still continues, but now it has grown to over 100 volunteers, food, a clothing give away, live music, a petting zoo, and free bikes for children who may never have a parent who could afford buying one. The owner of the strip mall always makes an appearance with a smile on his face. I asked him one year if he was okay with the obvious loss of business during our event, since it prevents his parking lot from being used for anything else. He just laughed and said he had 364 other days of the year to make a living. Carolyn has found her own Calcutta. All she had to do was lift up her eyes—it was there all along.

> *For we are His workmanship, created in Christ Jesus for good works, which God prepared beforehand that we should walk in them.*
>
> EPHESIANS 2:10

It is very easy for us to miss the divine setups that God places in our path. These can be right in front of us, and yet our own selfishness or sense of inconvenience can cloud us from seeing His greater purpose. I am a little embarrassed to admit that I have fallen into that trap many times. I am generally pretty clear on God's purpose for my own life. For many years my primary focus has been to try to reach as many people as possible with the life-changing message of the gospel. God has honoured that and has continually directed me by opening doors I would not have thought of if He had not presented the opportunities, like the television ministry story I told in chapter five. I have always tried to keep my head screwed on straight and keep things in proper perspective . . . it is not about me!

Having said this, I have had this resolve tested and I have not always passed. A few years ago, a friend called from rural Saskatchewan and asked if I would come and speak at their Christmas banquet. I really didn't want to do it. I was busy. It was inconvenient, and I tried to say no, but he wasn't really hearing me. In the end, I agreed to do it, but I was doing it begrudgingly. It was a lot of trouble. I had to catch an early morning flight, drive hours across the Saskatchewan prairie and then wait all day for the event to start. It turned out to be just a handful of people eating off of paper plates. This is going to sound dreadful, but I was thinking, *Don't these people know who I am? I'm a nationwide television celebrity and they've dragged me all the way out here for this.* Oh, I can hear you thinking right now that I am a dope, and you would be right. I had this terrible attitude the entire visit. That night I slept on my friend's couch, awoke at 3 AM in order to make my early morning flight out of Regina, and made it home in time to do our weekend services in Winnipeg. Although I never said anything out loud, I was grumbling in my heart the entire time.

Six months later, I received a letter from a woman in that town. Sue (not her real name) mentioned that she had come to the banquet and had brought her alcoholic husband. She was overjoyed to tell me that he had given his life to Christ that night. Not only had he become a Christian, he joined Alcoholics Anonymous, was attending the church, and had gotten water baptized. Sue went on to say that their marriage was restored and their entire family had made a miraculous turnaround. She was just writing me to thank me for "having such a great attitude" about coming to their "little banquet" in Saskatchewan. I should have been thrilled. And I was, for her and her family. But I couldn't get past the fact that I had been such a proud jerk when I was there. I realized that I had lost sight of my greater purpose, at least for that weekend.

NO ONE IS PUT ON PLANET EARTH WITHOUT A GOD-GIVEN DESTINY. TOO OFTEN WE DESPISE THE THINGS THAT ARE REALLY IMPORTANT AND VALUE THE THINGS THAT DON'T MATTER AT ALL.

The greatest fulfillment we get in life will never be what we do for ourselves but what we do for others. If I paint houses and my only motivation is to make enough money to get through another weekend, I will soon lose my interest in painting. If, on the other hand, I have a passion to create beautiful colour schemes that will bring joy to the heart of my client, that is a far more sustaining goal. If I am a mechanic and have no love of working on motors, I will be looking for a career change in no time. But if I have a passion to solve mechanical problems and see the relief on the face of my customer that his car is now running correctly, that is something worth getting up for in the morning.

When we establish objectives for our life, they need to come out of a sense of a greater and more meaningful purpose. No one is put on planet Earth without a God-given destiny. Too often we despise the things that are really important and value the things that don't matter at all.

> If anyone desires to come after me, let him deny himself, and take up his cross, and follow me. For whoever desires to save his life will lose it, but whoever loses his life for My sake will find it. For what profit is it to a man if he gains the whole world, and loses his own soul?
>
> MATTHEW 16:24–26

Many of us will spend our whole lives trying to gain the world, only to discover that we missed the mark completely. To truly follow Christ, you will have to deny self and take up your cross. It does not say to take up Jesus' cross, which was unique to him, but to take up our own cross. There is a common expression in our culture that states, "We all have our cross to bear." Typically, it is used in reference to one's mother-in-law, but in reality it has to do with the fact that we will all face a hardship that is unique to us. In bearing it, we will often find ourselves fulfilling our God-given destiny.

I am amazed at how many stay-at-home moms who have accepted the higher call of motherhood will dismiss it and say, "I'm just a stay-at-home mom." There is no such thing as JUST a stay-at-home mom! There is an old axiom that goes, "The hand that rocks the cradle rules the world." Thomas Edison said, "My mother was the making of me." Napoleon Bonaparte said, "The future destiny of a child is always the work of the mother."

Consider the story of Susanna Wesley. Born in 1669, she was the twenty-fifth of twenty-five children. Married at age nineteen to

Samuel Wesley, a Church of England pastor, they had nineteen children. Losing two in childbirth, she raised the surviving seventeen children almost singlehandedly. Presumably, being that she was pregnant nineteen times, her husband must have been around once in a while. Twice, the children burned down the house and she narrowly escaped losing more of them.

Susanna raised, educated and disciplined her children in such a manner that books are still being written about her methods today. Two of her children, John and Charles, revolutionized England in the 1700s. They are generally credited for the spiritual revival of the entire nation in their day. Charles was a great hymn writer who composed over 6,000 hymns and his brother John was the founder of the Methodist church. John travelled 250,000 miles on horseback, preached 40,000 times—three times a day for his entire adult life— and still managed to write over fifty volumes of books. The Methodist denomination that they founded has continued to grow worldwide for centuries after their passing. Although it is perhaps impossible to quantify the spiritual impact the Wesley's have made on our world, we can say that these brothers altered the course of human history. Having said that, we would be very remiss if we didn't give at least some of the credit to their mother Susanna, who deftly raised up two world-changing children.[6]

There is no such thing as JUST a housewife. Every one of us has a contribution to make to our world and the greatest tragedy would be to go through one's entire life and not realize that.

I have come to the conclusion that we are all called to live for a purpose greater than ourselves. It is impossible to find any trace of real fulfillment in living for oneself. Just look at the misery of those who spend their lives chasing fame and fortune. It is easily life's most empty pursuit.

Cecil Rhodes was one of history's wealthiest men. He established the De Beers diamond empire that at one time controlled 90% of the world's production. He had an entire country named after him—Rhodesia. He is as big a figure in African history as George Washington or John A. Macdonald is in ours. One day a newspaperman said to him, "You must be very happy."

Rhodes replied, "Happy?! No! I spent my life amassing a fortune, only to find I have spent half of it on doctors to keep me out of the grave, and the other half on lawyers to keep me out of jail!"[7]

WE ARE ALL CALLED TO LIVE FOR A PURPOSE GREATER THAN OURSELVES. IT IS IMPOSSIBLE TO FIND ANY TRACE OF REAL FULFILLMENT IN LIVING FOR ONESELF.

Christina Onassis was the daughter of Greek shipping magnate, Aristotle Onassis (who married Jackie Kennedy after the assassination of John F. Kennedy). Her brother died in a plane crash, her mother died of a drug overdose, she struggled with weight problems and pill popping of her own, and she married and divorced four times. In 1988, she died at the age of only thirty-seven and her three-year-old daughter, Athina, was dubbed the "richest little girl in the world." Christina is quoted in her biography, *All the Pain Money Can Buy*, as saying, "Happiness does not depend on money. Our family is the best proof of that."[8]

I could tell story after story like this, but it would just depress you.

True fulfillment will only come when we get our eyes off ourselves and onto others. I remember reading a story somewhere about a psychologist who developed a radical approach to dealing with depression in his patients. He would prescribe that they should, "Get up in the morning, wash your face and get dressed, walk across town and across the tracks and find someone in greater need than you. Help that person in any small way and you will be surprised at what it will do in you." He claimed many of his patients got free from their depression when they got their eyes off of themselves and realized that there is always someone worse off than them and everybody can make a difference.

Remember Don, the retiree at the beginning of the chapter? After he told me he was still looking for his "special purpose" (a cheeky reference to Steve Martin's movie *The Jerk*), he took me out fishing in the Gulf of Mexico. He owned a boat on the coast of Florida and wanted a chance to pick my brain about finding one's life purpose. I told him I could save him the price of the book and tell him in one sentence. One's greater purpose is always measured by what one does for others, not for oneself. Real fulfillment comes from making another fellow human being's life better. If we can figure out that one simple truth, and continue to apply it in different ways every single day, we will end up living a tremendously satisfying life. After I shared that with Don, I got an Amberjack on my line and we never pursued the conversation much farther.

Some months later, I ran into Don again, and he told me he had made a decision to live the rest of his life trying to make the lives of others better. He then said he had a lot of "pay back" to return and gave me a little wink. I am sure he was using the expression in the opposite sense of how we usually do. He told me that he had applied for a position as CEO of a non-profit organization that meets the needs of handicapped people. I could not have been more thrilled for Don, as it seemed he was well on his way to discovering his "special purpose."

There is a humorous Chinese proverb[10] that says:

> If you want to be happy for an hour—take a nap.
> If you want to be happy for a day—go fishing.
> If you want to be happy for a month—get married.
> If you want to be happy for a year—inherit a fortune.
> If you want to be happy for a lifetime—help someone else.

Chapter Twelve

Discovering Your Greater Purpose

You have not lived today until you have done something for someone who can never repay you.

— John Bunyon

FOR SOMETHING AS simple as serving others, our greater purpose is immensely elusive. The reason for that is we all have personal defaults. In computer terms, restoring to default means resetting to the original program. In human terms, it means we reset to our old ways and patterns of life. We so easily revert to the way we have always lived life, and for the most part, that will be both selfish and self-indulgent. The good news is that it is entirely possible to reprogram our lives.

In Matthew chapter 20 we have an intriguing story. Brothers John and James are escorted by their mother to Jesus' side, where she audaciously asks Him if it would be too much trouble for the boys to sit at His right and left hand when He comes into His kingdom. The other ten disciples were indignant upon hearing this. I think that they were just upset that their mothers hadn't thought of doing this first. But what makes the story interesting is Jesus' response:

But Jesus called them to Himself and said, "You know that the rulers of the Gentiles lord it over them, and those who are great exercise authority over them. Yet it shall not be so among you; but whoever desires to become great among you, let him be your servant. And whoever desires to be first among you, let him be your slave—just as the Son of Man did not come to be served, but to serve, and to give His life a ransom for many."

MATTHEW 20:25–28

Amazingly, Jesus does not rebuke their ambition for greatness but redefines it. He contrasts worldly greatness with kingdom greatness. We can either desire to rule over others or serve them. Things have not changed much in two thousand years. People with power still love to rule over those without. I am always amazed at the way we enjoy watching Donald Trump dispassionately dismiss failed contestants from his show *The Apprentice* with two curt words— "You're fired!" For me, he does it with far too much enjoyment.

Jesus, on the other hand, never put down or demeaned people. In fact, he was an "every man" kind of guy. He was a carpenter, a commoner who easily related to those He was trying to reach. But above all, He sought to serve them, even to the point of laying down His life. This was the example of greatness to which He encouraged His disciples to aspire, and it was James and John's for the taking.

It is hard to climb over the wall of "self-serving" to "others serving." However, I believe deep down within each one of us there is an empowering desire to do just that. We just need to discover how to tap into the specific God-given greater purpose that lies under the surface. The transformation happens as you 1) Realign your passions, 2) Reassign your gifting to God, and 3) Rediscover the joy of serving others.

1) REALIGN YOUR PASSIONS

Passion is one of life's most powerful forces. It is defined as an intense, driving, even overpowering, sense of conviction or desire. Scripture uses the words *desire* and *lust* almost interchangeably. Although we mostly think of lust in a negative way, it is a more apt word for passion since it connotes the intensity of the emotion. The apostle Paul used it to contrast the desires of flesh and spirit, saying, *"For the flesh lusts against the Spirit, and the Spirit against the flesh; and these are contrary to one another, so that you do not do the things that you wish"* (Galatians 5:17).

We are all familiar with fleshly passions, such as passion for sex, narcotics, food, money or pleasure. These passions have the power to rule over people's lives and enslave them. But passion is something God put within the human heart. It does not have to be negative. We can have passion for our jobs, our families and our hobbies.

When people tell me that they would like to get involved with the church or God's work and say they "just have no time," they are not being honest with themselves. We have all the time in the world for our personal passions. If our passion is cars, we can find time to wash them, wax them and work on them. If our passion is computer games, we will spend hours and hours on them. And golf is a borderline addiction that has created more orphans and widows than war.

> A man was seen on the golf course one day with four caddies. His golf buddies said, "Hey, George, what's with all the caddies?"
>
> George shouted back, "My wife thinks I should be spending more time with the kids!"

I also have many hobbies: snow skiing, waterskiing, windsurfing, fishing, boating, mechanics and carpentry, to name a few. Some of them border on obsession, and all of them are passions. As busy a man as I am, I always seem to be able to eke out time for my sports and hobbies. We make time for our passions!

King Solomon was a very passionate man. He had the entire kingdom of Israel to run, and yet he found time for 700 wives and 300 concubines. Or as my daughter once said, "300 porcupines! Who would want 300 porcupines?"

To which I said, "Who would want 700 wives?" (Or 700 in-laws, for that matter!)

Simply put, lack of time is an excuse. Our real problem is lack of passion. Maybe it would be better to say our real problem is lack of *meaningful* passion. The great secret to finding our greater purpose is to realign our passions with God's passions for us. By the end of King Solomon's life, he realized he had pursued the wrong passions:

> *Whatever my eyes desired I did not keep from them.*
> *I did not withhold my heart from any pleasure,*
> *For my heart rejoiced in all my labor;*
> *And this was my reward from all my labor.*
> *Then I looked on all the works that my hands had done*
> *And on the labor in which I had toiled;*
> *And indeed all was vanity and grasping for the wind.*
> *There was no profit under the sun . . .*
>
> *Therefore I hated life because the work that was done under*
> *the sun was distressing to me, for all is vanity and grasping for*
> *the wind.*
>
> ECCLESIASTES 2:10–11, 17

It is a great tragedy to discover that we spent our entire existence pursuing the wrong things. My fear is that many people will do exactly that with their one go-around. Discovering God's passion for your life is not as elusive as it seems. Psalm 37:4 gives us the answer. It says, *"Delight yourself also in the Lord, And He shall give you the desires of your heart."* Many misinterpret this to mean if we delight ourselves in the Lord, He will give us whatever our little heart desires. That is not what it is saying. It means that when we delight ourselves in God, the desires that enter our hearts are the ones He puts there. In other words, when we begin to focus our life on God, He gives us new desires that flow from the very throne room of heaven. Then, and only then, do we begin *"to lay hold of that for which Christ Jesus has also laid hold of me"* (Philippians 3:12b).

THE GREAT SECRET TO FINDING OUR GREATER PURPOSE
IS TO REALIGN OUR PASSIONS WITH GOD'S PASSIONS
FOR US.

I met Al about fifteen years ago. He was a very likable thirty-something-year-old bachelor with a good career but no responsibility for anyone other than himself. When he walked through the doors of our church, he had been a Christian for his entire life but had never really got involved beyond Sunday morning attendance. One weekend he heard me preach a message where I asked the question, "What do you do? We all have a contribution to make." Sitting there in the pew, he realized he had so much more to offer but had just never really availed himself. Right then and there, he volunteered to become an usher. He was a good usher— faithful, responsible—and could easily have taken over the role as head usher. But over time he realized he had a lot more he could contribute, and one day he signed up for a mission trip to Uganda.

That same year there was a sales contest at his place of work. He worked for a national food company that was going to take the top seven sales reps from across Canada, throw their names in a hat and select a winner who would receive a $15,000 Smart Car. By this point, Al had gotten married, and as the two of them were driving down the highway one day, he turned to Brenda, his wife, and said, "I'm going to win that car and I'm going to give the money to the Uganda project." Taking the $15,000 was an option instead of taking the car. That particular year, the mission team would be putting a power generator and water pump in an orphanage in a remote area and it was going to cost us $30,000 in total. Al ended up being the top sales rep for our local region and was invited to the big event in Toronto, where the seven finalists would wait to find out whose name was drawn.

When they drew Al's name, the CEO said to him, "You don't look very excited."

Al responded, "That's because I knew I was going to win and I would like to tell you what I am going to do with the money." He then explained the project and the CEO was so impressed, he offered to pay the travel costs for Al and Brenda to go with the team to Uganda. But Al wasn't done. He began to tell everyone that would listen that he would like to double the $15,000 to $30,000 and raise enough to pay for the entire project. Friends, family and co-workers all stepped up and Al raised every dime.

When he and the team left Uganda a few months later, he watched as the installed generator and water pump sent electricity and running water up the hill to the orphanage for the very first time. Suddenly, his job, his life and everything he lives for was put into perspective. He had gained a passion that transcended his career, his hobbies and most other things in his life. Today, he and his wife not only lead ministries in our church but also lead our trips to Uganda. They have been all over the world: Guatemala, Brazil, Zambia, Burkina Faso. Al still has his job as sales executive, but he does it with a new sense of passion because he has found a purpose greater than himself.

2) REASSIGN YOUR GIFTING TO GOD

Arnold Schwarzenegger is a name that almost everyone will recognize. He was the Terminator, then the Governator, and who knows what kind of 'nator he will be next. I have a pastor friend who calls himself the "Sermonator." I wish I had thought of that first! I am not sure how history will remember Schwarzenegger; it is hard to say at this point. But I bring him up because his name reminds me of Albert Schweitzer, one of my greatest heroes, and we do know how history remembers him. [1]

By the age of thirty, Albert Schweitzer was a success, no matter what methodology we might use to measure his accomplishments. He was a theologian, educator and musician. He wrote a number of books on religion, including *The Quest of the Historical Jesus*.[2] He was a teacher at the University of Strasbourg in Germany, and he was a much-respected principal of a small theological college. He taught university courses in religion, philosophy, and also Greek and Hebrew. Schweitzer was an outstanding church and concert organist; he even designed some of the world's greatest organs. In addition, he was an authority on the composer Johann Sebastian Bach and wrote several books about him.

In 1904, Schweitzer's life was forever altered by a seemingly innocent occurrence. His housekeeper had found a copy of the magazine *Paris Missionary* and left an article open on his desk entitled, "The needs of the Congo." It described the lack of workers in Gabon, the northern province of the Congo. After reading this article, Schweitzer felt empty about the direction of his life and decided right then and there that he would go to Africa and try to help the unfortunate people there. He knew he would do the most good if he could bring a significant skill to the mission field. He felt he could be most effective as a doctor.

Schweitzer enrolled in the University of Strasbourg medical school. His decision cost him his job and his place at the university. The stable, comfortable life he had built was lost, and his friends were unhappy that he hadn't consulted them. Even his mother couldn't understand his reasoning. His friends begged him to reconsider, saying, "Let someone else go. You have accomplished too much to just throw it all away and go to Africa." Schweitzer was beyond convincing and threw himself into his medical studies.

It was not until 1913 that he graduated from medical school. He immediately made arrangements to travel to Africa. He and his wife went to the city of Lambaréné in French Equatorial Africa, and he founded Schweitzer Hospital on the Ogooué River. Being on the river was vital because of the lack of roads in the jungle. The hospital needed to be easily accessible to villagers from all directions. People came to Dr. Schweitzer from the very first day, suffering from smallpox, leprosy, malaria, skin diseases, osteomyelitis and tropical dysentery. During the first nine months, 2,000 patients were treated. His very first hospital was in an old chicken house.

Schweitzer developed a personal philosophy he called "Reverence for Life." This was a basic belief that life was GOOD and should be preserved, promoted and raised to its highest value; it was bad to destroy, injure or repress it. He believed that any time even a plant or animal was to be killed, particular thought needed to be given to the eventual consequence of such an action. The African people took note of his profound conscientious nature and he gained great respect. Nevertheless, there were many challenges within the local customs in trying to bring healing to the natives. Witch doctors often tried to assign blame when someone died. Schweitzer had to go to great lengths to explain what had really happened in order to prevent revenge murders.

Because tradition meant that people were only to eat food prepared by their own families, he had to set up camps for the families to live nearby while medical treatment was taking place. Schweitzer established gardens and livestock farms in order to provide them with food to eat. By the end of his life, he had seventy-two buildings grouped around a central area. There was an operating theater, an X-ray room, a laboratory, a dental clinic, a delivery room, an outpatient clinic and a dispensary. The hospital did nearly 1,000 operations, with a death rate lower than the average in European hospitals. There were 6,000 patients treated every year.

In 1952, the world took notice and Schweitzer was awarded the Nobel Peace Prize. He instantly became very famous and known the world over. His hospital became a popular tourist stop. Schweitzer rejected many offers from corporations offering to provide financial help to the hospital. While such aid would have meant a more modern hospital, he was afraid he might lose control and that patient-care would suffer. In Schweitzer's mind, the patients always came first.

Schweitzer was more gifted than most of us could ever dream to be, and yet, he reassigned that gifting to serve God. In doing so, he discovered his greater purpose.

I am always cautious about using such dramatic examples because we mere mortals have a hard time relating to Nobel Prize winners. The point is not to try to aspire to their level but to try to apply the principle to where we live every day. We all have giftings that we must be willing to reassign from personal gain to use for the greater glory of God. It doesn't matter how grand or miniscule it might look like on the surface; we all have something to offer the greater good.

Ivan is one of our church board members. He is a lawyer by profession and has a keen mind. He brings his considerable talents to the table when we are grinding out increasingly difficult policy decisions in a complicated, regulation-saturated world. I could tell you all about how he has dedicated that gifting to God's service, but again it would be more inaccessible then most of us can relate to. So, let me tell you about Ivan's other interest. He is a bike guy. He has all the tools and a fancy stand to work on bikes. Over the last few years, Ivan has headed up the bike ministry in our church. We have a shop in the back of our building with hundreds of used bikes hanging from racks. Originally, we got permission from the city to collect them from the landfill site. Today, people know what we do and donations come in weekly. Ivan and his team spend every Wednesday night refurbishing these bikes into perfectly working, often new-looking, vehicles. In the spring and summer of the year, they head into Winnipeg's inner city and put them in the hands of economically disadvantaged children—kids whose parents would probably never be able to afford to give their children a new bike. The smiles on the faces of those kids are all the reward Ivan needs. Most people in the church would not know it is a lawyer who has dedicated that kind of time and talent to ensure a better life for inner city children. Ivan is touching his greater purpose because he has reassigned his gifting to God.

3) REDISCOVER THE JOY OF SERVING OTHERS.

In 1953, after Albert Schweitzer received the Nobel Peace Prize, he was invited to the United States on a speaking tour. He arrived in

Chicago by train and there were reporters, city officials and well-wishers waiting for him. As he stepped off the train, he was greeted by flash bulbs, smiling faces and a throng of people. But he didn't immediately speak to the waiting crowd; instead, he appeared to be looking over the heads of the crowd. He was an imposing figure of a man—standing over 6'4" tall with bushy eyebrows and moustache—and could easily have been intimidating.

"Excuse me just a moment," he said, and he made his way through the crowd. He came to an elderly black lady who was having trouble carrying two suitcases. He walked over and said, "Let me help you, Ma'am." He picked up the suitcases, walked with her all the way through the terminal, put the suitcases on a bus and wished her a nice day. He then turned around to face the reporters and city officials who had followed him, many of them who were oddly pretending to be looking for other passengers to help, and said, "Excuse me. I'm sorry I made you wait." It was not a pretense. This was who Schweitzer was. It was a living sermon of what this man was all about—serving others.[3]

Jesus was very clear on this point. The greatest of all is the servant of all. This is completely contrary to everything we see from the so-called great people of our day, or any day, but it remains the true measure of greatness. Of course, we would never serve others out of the selfish motive of desiring greatness. There is, however, a certain reward that is undeniable. Social scientists sometimes call it the law of social reciprocity; we help others because of the benefit of feeling better about ourselves. I personally consider that a by-product, not a motivation. Still, Scripture teaches the joy of giving and serving:

> *Looking unto Jesus, the author and finisher of our faith, <u>who</u>*
> <u>*for the joy that was set before Him*</u> *endured the cross, despising*

the shame, and has sat down at the right hand of the throne of God.

HEBREWS 12:2, *emphasis added*

Life takes on new meaning when we rediscover the joy of serving others. To help individuals in our church find their greater purpose, one of the things we do is send them on a short-term mission trip. It puts people in a place where they have to (get to) serve people who will never be able to repay them. It is in this environment, sequestered from our familiar culture, that we learn the joy of serving others. Over the years we have sent teams to literally hundreds of places, like Mexico, Haiti, Uganda and the Philippines. We are under no illusions that someone can go to a developing nation for a week or two or even three and really make any lasting difference. The lasting benefit will almost always come in the transformation of the people we send.

Those who have lived their entire lives in the affluent and comfortable West return from a short-term mission trip with a whole new set of values regarding what is really important as well as a new understanding of how immeasurably blessed they are. Most of them become lifelong partners in the missions work we do around the world. The true lasting benefit of this is not easily quantified, but it is significant. For example, at this writing, our congregation is fully funding five translation projects among unreached people groups.[‡] Because of the mission-mindedness of our people, they willingly fund these projects to the tune of hundreds of thousands of dollars.

In 2014, the Aringa people in Uganda received a Bible in their language. It was a twelve-year project that finished three years ahead

---

[‡] An unreached people group is defined as an ethno-linguistic group that does not have a Bible in their own language or a credible gospel witness to their culture. There are some 2,500 of these groups remaining that have still not heard the good news about Jesus.

of schedule. Because the Aringa did not have a written language, they were almost 100% illiterate, a prescription for poverty in our day and age. The translation project, which was done through the Wycliffe Global Alliance, not only produced a New Testament but books on hygiene and other essential day-to-day aspects of life. For the first time in their history, 25,000 Aringa children are in school learning to read and write. Their main textbook is the Bible. It is even more significant when you realize that the tribe is almost entirely non-Christian.

We may not have been able to do these projects if many of our people had not been to the developing world and seen the need. It is hard not to feel a sense of joy to be part of something so significant, even if it is only in some small way. My favourite quote from Mother Teresa is, "Don't look for big things, just do small things with great love . . . The smaller the thing, the greater must be our love."[4]

We do not need to cross an ocean, of course, to discover our greater purpose. If we realign our passions with the Lord's, reassign our giftings to God and rediscover the joy of serving others, we will have already gone a long way to finding the ultimate destiny for our life.

Chapter Thirteen

The Lost Art of Contentment

The world is full of people looking for spectacular happiness while they snub contentment.

— Doug Larson[1]

The good life exists only when you stop wanting a better one. It is the condition of savouring what is, rather than longing for what may be. The itch for things—so brilliantly injected by those that make and sell them—is in effect the virus draining the soul of contentment.

— Marya Mannes[2]

WHILE I AM on the subject of visiting the developing world, I should bring up the subject of contentment. If we never achieve any sense of contentment in life, we will be continually searching for the pot of gold at the end of the rainbow and our greater purpose will likely elude us.

We live in a culture of discontentment. We are told every day that we should not be satisfied with what we have. Advertising has figured out a way to make us feel discontent, telling us that we will just not be happy in life if we do not have the latest car, TV or stereo. And Lord help you if you have the wrong cell phone!

For years they told us the smaller the cell phone, the better. We were approaching the Dick Tracey watch phone when the trend reversed, and now it is the smarter the phone, the better. Not only did they get smarter, but they got bigger. People are now carrying cellphones the size of a coffee table.

This culture of discontentment produces insatiable desire. You can never be satisfied because the next greatest thing comes along and you are right back there again wanting . . . desiring . . . no, needing. If that is where you live, you need a little dose of the developing world.

IF WE NEVER ACHIEVE ANY SENSE OF CONTENTMENT IN LIFE, WE WILL BE CONTINUALLY SEARCHING FOR THE POT OF GOLD AT THE END OF THE RAINBOW AND OUR GREATER PURPOSE WILL LIKELY ELUDE US.

One of the places we have travelled to do missions work is Matamoras, Mexico. This is a border city right across the Rio Grande from Brownsville, Texas. Today in Mexico, the drug cartels have taken complete control of the border cities. They have become incredibly violent places where, on a bad weekend, 100 murders can take place. The cartels want these cities because they are the smuggling portals into the United States.

There is a big movement growing in Canada and the US to legalize marijuana. Proponents say it is a harmless recreational drug and not at all dangerous like harder drugs. What they fail to mention is that fifty percent of Mexico's drug exports are cannabis. It is the bread and butter for the cartels, and legalizing it on this side of the border will merely increase demand. They have no objection with where public sentiment is heading. The unfortunate consequence for us is that it is no longer safe for us to go into places where our church has worked for twenty-five years.

When we used to go into Matamoras, we worked with a husband and wife pastoral team, Anna and Timoteo. They have been doing a great work there, and despite the violence, they continue to plug away at it. As a church we sponsored 135 children who got to go to school because we supplied them with uniforms, school supplies and tuition. Without these items, they would never have had an opportunity for an education.

When we would arrive in Matamoras, I would always try my best to speak my very inadequate Spanish. "Buenos días me hermano en Cristo, como esta?" I would say to Timoteo.

And he would always respond, "Buenos días, Estoy contento," which is to say, "Good morning, I am content." Rarely would he use the more jubilant "Estoy feliz." Even if you do not speak Spanish, you will recognize this word from the seasonal greeting, "Feliz Navidad," or "Merry Christmas." *Feliz* means happy. Cookies make us happy. Good fortune makes us happy. Christmas and birthdays are a time for merriment and *feliz*. Timoteo does not live in *feliz* every day, but he is content. This is remarkable, because compared to you and me, Timoteo has almost nothing. Both of us are pastors, and neither of us chose where to live, we were just born there. I was born into the upper-middle-class world and he was born into the developing world. I am continually dissatisfied with what I possess, yet he is *contento*.

We can tend to feel sorry for people in the developing world who do not have the conveniences of the Western world, but most of the time, we should not. One of the things you discover as you travel is that, usually, these people are not unhappy. They may not even have a job or much in the way of possessions, but they have their families and their friends, and if they get food on the table once a day they are content.

The last time we were in Matamoras, we were travelling 200 km to the city of Mante (pronounced "Monty") to do a gospel meeting. We had dubbed the campaign "The Full Monty." Timoteo wanted me to ride with him in his car. He was so proud of the fact that he even had a car. An American missionary had given it to him. It was a 1974 Crown Victoria. The brakes were shot, the shocks were toast and blue smoke billowed out the exhaust when he drove. The rest of our team would ride in our air-conditioned fifteen-passenger van, but I would ride with Timoteo and Anna. His car has "4/60" air conditioning—four windows down at sixty miles per hour.

It was 35°C that morning as we drove down the highway. I was grateful we did not have to travel through a mountain pass. They are harrowing at the best of times, and I cannot imagine the journey with marginal brakes. After driving only about a half-hour, we pulled off the road. I asked why we were stopping and Timoteo pointed to the engine temperature gauge—which was pinned at the top of the dial—and laughed. We waited for about ten minutes for the radiator to cool. He then went to the trunk and grabbed two gallon milk jugs full of water. After replenishing the radiator, we drove for another half-hour till we stopped and did it all again. A trip that should have taken three hours, tops, took us close to six hours.

We rolled into a gas station in Mante on fumes. I told Timoteo I would pay for the gas. He respectfully asked if he could top up the oil as well. I watched as he added one litre, then another, then a third. He checked the dipstick, which was halfway to full and said, "Bueno." It had just taken 3 of a possible 4.5 litres of oil.

If we owned a car like this, most of us would complain about our poverty every opportunity we got. Timoteo feels like a millionaire because he actually owns a car. If I owned a car like this, I would drive it straight into the river without giving it a second thought.

Many of us could quote Philippians 4:13 by memory: *"I can do all things through Christ who strengthens me."* It is a triumphal and victorious verse that makes us feel like there is no mountain too high, no river too wide or no beast too ferocious that we could not conquer it. The problem is that this is not really what the verse is talking about. One must always read Scripture in context. It reads this way:

> *Not that I speak in regard to need, for I have learned in whatever state I am, to be content: I know how to be abased, and I know how to abound. Everywhere and in all things I have learned both to be full and to be hungry, both to abound and to suffer need. I can do all things through Christ who strengthens me.*
>
> PHILIPPIANS 4:11–13

This passage is about contentment. The apostle Paul says that he has *learned* to be content in whatever situation he finds himself. Whether he has abundance or suffers lack, he will remain content. If he has food or goes hungry, it doesn't matter, for he *can do all things through Christ who strengthens him.* That puts a completely different spin on the passage. Our greater purpose seems intrinsically connected to our ability to learn contentment in whatever situation God has placed us.

After Albert Schweitzer won the Nobel Prize, he was still working tirelessly in the Congo. One day, the Governor General came to pay him a visit. Schweitzer thought he had better look his best, so he put on his black tie. His assistant objected and told him that he could not wear that tie because it was old and very worn.

Schweitzer responded, "I can't imagine why. I have had it only eighteen years and I have it only to wear to christenings and funerals."

"Eighteen years!" his assistant exclaimed incredulously, "Don't you have another, a second tie?"

"Fortunately not," he said, "my father had two, and I remember how they were always looking for the better tie."[3]

OUR GREATER PURPOSE SEEMS INTRINSICALLY CONNECTED TO OUR ABILITY TO LEARN CONTENTMENT IN WHATEVER SITUATION GOD HAS PLACED US.

If you were to survey what the preachers on television are preaching (and yes, I realize I am one of them and I have my own critics), you would discover that what many of them serve up is not a whole lot different than the world's best motivational speakers. They talk about victory and success and lots about happiness. Their messages are very encouraging, and for the most part, will work if applied circumspectly to one's life. My objection is that many of them are indistinguishable from the self-help, human potential gurus like Anthony Robbins (who never ever mentions the need for God). An observer from outer space might get the idea that Christianity is a prescription for health, wealth and unbridled happiness. My contention is that this is not what the Bible promises.

The early church, in particular, endured intense persecution. It was not uncommon for their meetings to be raided and their leaders murdered as they watched. Both Stephen and James were publically martyred. The Church of Jerusalem was scattered abroad as a result, in what became known as the Christian Diaspora (dispersion). Many of the epistles were written to those Christians that were dispersed.

Peter, an apostle of Jesus Christ, To the pilgrims of the Dispersion in Pontus, Galatia, Cappadocia, Asia, and Bithynia . . .

1 PETER 1:1

The message of these letters was not that they should become obscenely successful entrepreneurs in their new homelands but that they should have joy and contentment in the midst of hardship and persecution. These Christians were encouraged that what the world offered paled in comparison to the salvation of their souls and what they had in Christ. Peter and Paul continually inspired them to keep their priorities straight and to learn to be content in whatever situation they found themselves. Peter writes in his first epistle,

> *In this you greatly rejoice, though now for a little while, if need be, you have been grieved by various trials, that the genuineness of your faith, being much more precious than gold that perishes, though it is tested by fire, may be found to praise, honor, and glory at the revelation of Jesus Christ, whom having not seen you love. Though now you do not see Him, yet believing, you rejoice with joy inexpressible and full of glory, receiving the end of your faith—the salvation of your souls.*
>
> 1 PETER 1:6–9

When was the last time you heard a message preached on these verses? I had an interesting discussion on this one day with my friend Greg. Greg works for an organization called Voice of the Martyrs (VOM). VOM was founded in the 1960s by Richard Wurmbrand, who was imprisoned for faith in Christ for fourteen years in Communist Romania. His wife, Sabina, was also imprisoned for three years. They were ransomed out of Romania and came to North America and began the ministry to assist other Christians around the world who are persecuted for their faith. Greg has travelled the world and gone into places where sharing your faith is a crime punishable by death. The believers in these countries live a very different Christianity than we do. Their churches do not meet openly but underground, in homes, unmarked buildings or merely in rice paddies.

I noticed one day that Greg had started to attend our church with his family instead of his regular home church. I told him he was welcome but wanted to know why, after all these years of being friends, he was just now deciding that he wanted to be part of our congregation. He made this comment: "After travelling to some of the most restrictive nations in the world, I decided that the genuine gospel should work in any nation in the world. And if what we preach will only work in the affluent West, I have to ask myself if that is the whole counsel of God? I believe, Mark, that your preaching, if you can get past the Bart Simpson references, would work anywhere in the world." That may possibly be the highest compliment anyone has ever paid me. But more importantly, I think it is a realization that more people need to come to. The Bible does teach success and prosperity—but not as the greatest objectives of our faith. Character, honesty, integrity, virtue, compassion, faithfulness, endurance, perseverance, persistence, obedience, heroism, sacrifice, servanthood, kindness and humility are all higher aspirations.

The apostle Paul spends far more time talking about his adversities then he ever does his victories. For him, the measurement of faith would be net perseverance, not net profit. Again and again, we hear the call to contentment. He encourages his young protégé Timothy with these words,

> *Now godliness with contentment is great gain. For we brought nothing into this world, and it is certain we can carry nothing out. And having food and clothing, with these we shall be content.*
>
> 1 TIMOTHY 6:6–8

Aleksandr Solzhenitsyn, the Russian dissident and author of *The Gulag Archipelago*,[4] spent eight years in Russian imprisonment camps. His crime was criticizing Joseph Stalin in a letter to a friend. During his time in forced labour, he found Christ as his Lord and Saviour. He recalled how that experience changed his perspective entirely concerning his situation. As long as he tried to maintain some pitiful degree of worldly power over his situation, food, clothing, etc., he was constantly under the heel of his captors. But after his conversion, when he surrendered himself powerless, he discovered he inexplicably became free of even his captors.

If you are in Christ, you are free, regardless of your circumstances. Freedom, and consequently contentment, come from Him and not from your circumstances. Incidentally, Paul was in prison himself when he wrote, *"for I have learned in whatever state I am, to be content"* (Philippians 4:11). If Paul the apostle can find contentment in prison, if Aleksandr Solzhenitsyn can find contentment in the Gulag, and if my poor pastor friend Timoteo can find contentment in Matamoras, Mexico, then surely every one of us should be able to find contentment in our affluent culture of abundance. There is something liberating about looking at the place God has positioned us in life and realizing that He has put us there for a cause greater than ourselves. If God is sovereign (and He is), then every one of us are uniquely positioned to discover our greater purpose wherever we are.

Someone once said there are really only two rules in life: 1) Don't sweat the small stuff; and 2) It's all small stuff. Looking at the big picture allows us to not sweat the small stuff.

I have repeated over and over through these chapters that our greater purpose and personal happiness are two very different things. Although I would never want to deny anyone a slice of happiness in life, our destinies exist on a much higher plain—or a lower plain, depending on how you look at it. The New Testament repeatedly shares concepts such as "the way up is down," "less is more," and "the greatest is the least." If we get trapped in the upwardly mobile materialism of our culture, we may miss opportunities to do something meaningful with our lives.

> *Believe, when you are most unhappy, that there is something for you to do in the world. So long as you can sweeten another's pain, life is not in vain.*
>
> — Helen Keller

Chapter Fourteen

The Seeds of Success

Every failure brings with it the seed of an equivalent success.
— Napoleon Hill

BY THIS POINT we have pretty good idea what our *greater purpose* should look like and how we need to refocus our lives to start moving toward it. The challenge becomes this: life is not linear. We rarely have the luxury of moving from A to B to C, and so forth, in a straight line. Life dishes out all kinds of detours, ditches, roadblocks, derailments and sometimes train wrecks. None of these things mean God's plan for our life has changed. In fact, these very things are part of the plan. God, in His sovereignty, knows the beginning from the end and weaves even life's most difficult moments into His greater scheme. The biggest difficulty is our inability to see the big picture.

It is true that within every failure lies the seed of success, yet it is a principle that few of us recognize exists, let alone embrace. I will expand on this concept, but first there is a corollary to this principle that we think about even less, and that is "within every success lie the seeds of failure."

Motorola is a great example of how success can sow the seeds for future misfortune. In 2003, they came out with the Motorola Razr cell phone. It was a thin and handsome phone and much more appealing than the clunky Nokia phones that had been the market leaders at the time. Demand for the phone took off, and within a year, it was the top selling clamshell phone and within a hair of overtaking Nokia's worldwide sales. A company vice-president boasted that nobody was going to be able to catch them now. That's always a first sign of impending disaster, since "pride goes before a fall." Motorola's success was to be short-lived, ironically, as the trend was not going to be for cell phones to get smaller, but bigger. While Motorola and Nokia were duking it out for market share, RIM and Apple and others were quietly working on smarter phones, not smaller. The Blackberry, and later the Apple iPhone, hit the market with a vengeance. Within three years, Motorola fell from market leader to market laggard. By 2008, they had a market share of only 6% and lost $3.6 billion in one year.[1]

As paradoxical as this sounds, success is sometimes the very worst thing that can happen to us. Success can make us lazy, complacent and soft. Millions of people think that if they could just win the lottery all of their troubles in life would be over. Nothing could be farther from the truth. I am always amazed at how many people will line up in front of the kiosks to buy lottery tickets. I lovingly refer to lotteries as "the tax on the stupid." They seem to have no idea that their chances of winning are about the same as being picked for the space program. More importantly, they do not know that even if they do win, chances are higher that it will ruin their life rather than fix it.

SUCCESS IS SOMETIMES THE VERY WORST THING THAT CAN HAPPEN TO US.

I made a proposal to the producer of our television show to pitch an idea for a reality show to the networks called "Million Dollar Losers." It would follow the lives of lottery winners as they spiral out of control. There is no shortage of real life stories.

In 1988, William "Bud" Post won $16.2 million in the Pennsylvania state lottery. He had hit the mother lode and it was going to be easy street from here on in. He quit his job, like they almost all do, and started spending money like a drunken sailor. His first setback came when a former girlfriend successfully sued him for a half share of his winnings. Rather than being happy for Bud, his brother was arrested for hiring a hit man to kill him, hoping to inherit a share of the winnings. His other siblings were only a little more subtle and pestered Post until he agreed to invest in their business ideas. One was a car business and the other a restaurant in Sarasota, Florida. Both ventures failed. Within only one year of winning over $16 million, he was now $1 million in debt. Things only got worse from there, as he was sent to jail for firing a gun over the head of a bill collector. Around the same time, he declared bankruptcy. When he did emerge from jail, he was penniless and unemployed. Today, he lives quietly on $450 a month and food stamps. Post sums up the experience this way, "I wish it never happened. It was totally a nightmare."[2]

I know no one ever believes that they would be that stupid. When I tell stories like that, people say, "Well, I think I would do fine winning the lottery. I would still like to give it a try." It's like the guy that won $10 million in the lottery and was asked by the newspaper how he did it.

"I'd have to say it was half brains and half luck. My favourite number is 11. So I picked 11 + 11, which equals 23 for my numbers. And sure enough, the winning numbers were 11, 11, 23."

Perplexed, the reporter said, "But 11 + 11 equals 22."

"I know," said the man, "that was the lucky part."

Within every success lies the seed of failure. Sometimes success is the worst thing that can happen to you. Now for the good news:

within every failure lies the seed of success. That means there is hope for the rest of us.

Nobody likes pain and suffering. Most of us spend our entire lives trying to avoid it. We prefer comfort and prosperity. We have trouble seeing any good in hardship at all, but the fact is, it is suffering and failure that are the true seeds of success.

Dr. Paul Brand authored a fascinating book entitled, *Pain: The Gift Nobody Wants.*[3] He wrote this oddly titled book from the context of being a surgeon who worked for years among leprosy patients in Africa. He saw firsthand the devastating effects that come upon people who lack pain—damaged feet, fingers, noses, or eyes, often leading to infection, misery and death.

I have had the dubious honour of visiting a leper colony in India. I don't know of a more heartwrenching sight than a group of people living together whose bodies have been ravaged by leprosy. Fingers, toes, noses and ears missing, oozing wounds wrapped in puss soaked rags. The closest thing I can use to describe the scene is that of a zombie movie. Lepers were actually considered the walking dead for centuries.

Dr. Brand points out that it is not the leprosy itself that causes the loss of the body parts but the fact that lepers lose sensitivity in their nerve endings and therefore lose the sensation of pain. Most of the damage to their bodies is self-inflicted from stepping on sharp objects, being burned by hot objects or other common accidents. Without the reflex of pain, they continually expose themselves to hazards that we would naturally avoid. It is hard to imagine, but we rely on the gift of pain every single day to keep us out of harm's way. It is pain that tells us when to stop an activity that is starting to damage our body. It could be as simple as a blister on your hand as you are swinging a hammer or the reflex of waiting to drink coffee that is too hot. For all of our avoidance of pain, it may be one of God's greatest gifts to us, in more ways than one.

The reality is that we accomplish far more through pain and suffering than we ever will through comfort and ease. Almost all progress comes as a result of failure. When a situation becomes so bad that it is no longer tolerable, someone will always respond to the need and bring change. That is why "necessity is the mother of invention." Complacency never produces anything, but pain, suffering and need always do.

It was Canadian Henry Woodward who actually invented the electrical light bulb. He found he could only get it to illuminate for a few moments before the filament burned out. He incorrectly assumed that there was no future for such a capricious device and sold the patent to someone with more foresight and patience—Thomas Edison. Soon afterwards, Edison developed the tungsten filament that is still in use today. Edison's perseverance in the face of failure is legendary. When he was trying to develop the nickel-iron battery, he laboured for five months without success. A young colleague commented, "It's a shame that we should have worked all these weeks without getting any results!"

Edison reacted in surprise, "No results? Why, man, I have gotten a lot of results! I know several thousand things that won't work."[4]

There are countless stories throughout history where the seeds of success were planted in failure. Since I am on the sowing/reaping theme, let me give you a couple of agricultural examples.

In the first part of the 20th century, Enterprise, Alabama, was a community based on growing cotton. It was a bread and butter crop, and for the most part, that is all they grew. For many years they had excellent harvests. Those from farming backgrounds will recognize that any time farmers fail to rotate their crops they run the risk of developing disease and insect problems. In 1815, they had a Mexican boll weevil infestation that destroyed 60% of their cotton harvest. The next year, they planted everything to cotton again with the perennial hope that you hear in farmers' voices when they say, "Well, there is always next year." Except, in Enterprise, there was no next year. The cotton was once again devastated by the boll weevil.

In 1917, they knew they needed to do something different and many of them planted peanuts for the first time. They turned out to be hardy and completely resistant to the boll weevil. The county produced more peanuts than any other in America that year. The crop was so profitable that those who managed not to go broke found themselves out of debt and agriculture in the region was reborn. In 1919, the citizens of Enterprise got together and erected a monument to the boll weevil, dubbing it "The Herald of Prosperity." The base of the monument is inscribed: "In profound appreciation of the Boll Weevil and what it has done as the Herald of Prosperity this monument was erected by the Citizens of Enterprise, Coffee County, Alabama." The Boll Weevil Monument is a symbol of man's willingness and ability to adjust to adversity. To this day, the people of Enterprise talk about the boll weevil being the best thing that ever happened to them.[5]

In 1872, vineyard owner William Thompson of Sutter County, California, imported a Sultanina seedless grape cutting. The seedless grape turned out to be a hit with consumers. His prescience was also rewarded when the Sultanina was his only vine to survive sudden winter floods. The following year, the region was devastated by drought and the grapes literally shrivelled on the vine. They were harvested anyway and shipped to San Francisco, where an enterprising merchant sold them as "Peruvian delicacies." Thompson seedless grapes became the basis of California's raisin industry.[6] The series of misfortunes turned out to be the best thing to ever happen to Sutter County. Within every failure lie the seeds of success—never mind that the grapes had no seeds.

This principle is perhaps one of the hardest for us to grasp. It is hard to get excited about adversity, failure and hardship. But if we can learn to *"count it all joy when you fall into various trials, knowing that the testing of your faith produces patience"* (James 1:2–4), there is no telling what good can come out of the situation. Let's be honest about it; nobody enjoys hardship. We would all prefer a charmed life, but it is not going to happen so we had better embrace the alternative.

I think one of Canada's most inspiring heroes is Rick Hansen. Rick was born and raised in British Columbia. As a youth, he was a super athlete and excelled in every sport he took up. In 1973, at the age of fifteen, his life took a dramatic turn. He was carelessly riding in the back of a pickup truck when it swerved off the road and hit a tree. Rick was thrown from the truck bed. He suffered a spinal injury and has been paralyzed for the waist down ever since. His love for sport never diminished, and after completing high school, he enrolled in the University of British Columbia. There, he became the first student with a physical disability to ever graduate with a degree in Physical Education. He became a Paralympian, winning three golds, two silvers and one bronze medal. He also won nineteen wheelchair marathons, of which three were world championships.

Like many other Canadians, Rick was inspired by the heroic effort of Terry Fox to run across Canada raising money for cancer research. In 1980, Terry's run was cut short by the return of his bone cancer. By 1981, Terry had succumbed to his disease and passed away. Rick decided that he would take up a similar challenge to raise funds for spinal cord research. In 1985, he embarked on his Man in Motion tour, which was essentially a plan to wheelchair around the world. Departing from Vancouver in March of that year, Rick logged 40,000 kilometers over the next twenty-six months. He travelled through thirty-four countries, on four different continents. After two years on the road, he had surpassed his $1 million goal and had raised over $26 million for spinal cord research. Today, the Rick Hansen Foundation has raised over $200 million dollars.

I remember reading what Rick said when he was being interviewed during the twenty-fifth anniversary of his tour. He said something that I will never forget as long as I live: "You go back to the days of a 15-year-old kid in a hospital bed with a shattered spine and told you'll never walk again, thinking your hopes and dreams were gone and not to have too much hope because there wouldn't be much out there. And to be able to compare that to this moment knowing that I'm one of the luckiest guys on the planet and I'd never, ever trade my life for the use of my legs."[7] Wow, if Rick Hansen can get to the point where he not only does not regret his tragedy but embraces it as defining him and making him a better person, then every one of us should be able to see the seeds of success that lie within every one of our failures, struggles and hardships.

In Genesis 37, we learn that Joseph was the second-youngest of Jacob's twelve sons. Because he was born during his father's old age, Joseph was spoiled and treated more like a grandson than a son. On top of that his father made him a "*coat of many colours*" (Genesis 37:3). The multicolored tunic was a robe of distinction that was usually reserved for the eldest, not one of the youngest.

Most of us have witnessed how last-born children get treated in families. The eldest are given all the rules, the most demands put on them and all the chores. When the youngest comes along, the parents are usually sick of the hassle and throw the rules out the window and raise them in a completely different manner. My two eldest children always complain about how our youngest had it so easy. I don't really care about their complaints, and I will dismissively say, "Well, you should have thought about that before you decided to be born first."

Or, sometimes I will say, "Life isn't fair and neither am I, so get used to it!" That statement is far truer than they believe.

Joseph did have it way too easy. He paraded around in his prestigious garment while his brothers' hatred for him grew every day. Then came the pivotal point in Joseph's life. He had a couple of dreams: one with eleven wheat sheaves (his brothers) bowing down to his wheat sheaf, and another of the sun, moon (his father and mother) and the eleven stars (his brothers) all bowing down to him. In his naïve and youthful excitement, he failed to realize that his family would not share his enthusiasm for the dreams. They instead looked at each other and said, "Let's kill him!" In the end, they sold him off as a slave in Egypt, where he ended up in Potiphar's house. As far as slaves went, Joseph was very successful—maybe too successful. Potiphar's wife had eyes for him. When he rebuffed her seduction, she cried "rape" and Joseph found himself in prison. So far, things did not really go as planned. He went from favourite son to slave, and now, to prisoner.

Amazingly, Joseph did not lose heart but seemed to have a knack for making the best of every situation. While he was in prison, the Bible actually says of him, *"The Lord was with him; and whatever he did, the Lord made it prosper"* (Genesis 39:23). Joseph gained a reputation for interpreting dreams while in the "big house." When the Pharaoh had a particularly disturbing dream, they called on Joseph to interpret it, which he did. The dream was about seven fat cows, which represented seven plentiful years, and seven skinny cows, which represented seven drought years that were to follow. When Joseph recommended a plan to store grain during the seven good years in order to survive the seven bad years, the Pharaoh was so impressed that he put him in charge. In fact, Joseph became the most powerful man in Egypt, next to the Pharaoh. Quite the reversal of fortune!

As it turned out, the famine not only affected Egypt but Israel as well. Eventually Joseph's brothers ended up in Egypt looking for help and found themselves bowing down right at his feet. They did not recognize their long lost brother and Joseph messed with their heads for a bit first. Then he demanded they return with their father and younger brother, Benjamin. Upon their return, all thirteen bowed down at his feet, just like the dream had predicted.

After he revealed his identity, his brothers expressed great sorrow for the way they had treated Joseph years ago. Joseph's answer reveals his hidden *greater purpose* within the story, *"But now, do not therefore be grieved or angry with yourselves because you sold me here; for God sent me before you to preserve life"* (Genesis 45:5). Had Joseph's brothers not mistreated him, the course of events that spared all of Israel would not have transpired.

God, in His divine providence, has not lost control of our lives when things don't go our way. In fact, it is just the opposite. We do not succeed in life *despite* our failures; we succeed *because* of them. Within every failure lies the seed of success. Our greater purpose is rarely found in our victories but hidden within the struggles and even the abject failures of our journey.

Most people would not be surprised to hear that, as a young man, I probably suffered from a case of overconfidence. By the time I was in my twenties, I had a brash confidence that there was nothing I could not do and no giant I could not defeat. After Kathy and I were married, we agreed that we would not live on the family farm, which I had been running for the previous several years. I never grew up on a farm, but my father had purchased it as he always had this thing for the land. After graduating high school, I ran the farm for him while I was going through university. It was a great experience for me, as I learned so many different skills. Farmers are not simple country folks anymore but agronomists, mechanics, welders, electricians, builders, bookkeepers, futures traders, grain marketers and the list goes on and on. My ten years on the farm taught me all those things and more. So, when we took up residence in Winnipeg as a young married couple, I assumed employers would be tripping over themselves to hire me. I am almost embarrassed to admit this, but unlike most normal people looking for a job who drop off applications with the personnel department, I was phoning companies and making appointments with the presidents. Timid, I was not! However I got shot down in interview after interview by perplexed company executives who wondered why I was there in the first place.

One such encounter became a defining moment in my life. I was sitting in the president's office at Pioneer Grain, in the prestigious Richardson Building at the corner of Portage and Main in Winnipeg. Across his big oak desk, he asked me why I "needed" to see him. I explained I was looking for a job, to which he asked what I did now.

When I responded, "Well, nothing at the moment," he asked what my wife did. I repeated, "Well, nothing at the moment."

He replied with a somewhat condescending, but accurate, "You really do need a job!"

When he asked what I could do for his company, I arrogantly (and there is no other way to say it) claimed, "I can do anything you want me to do."

To which he retorted, "That would be up to me to determine, now wouldn't it?"

About that moment, I felt like a complete loser and was wondering myself what I was doing there. He politely handed me the card of the personnel manager and mentioned that he had heard they were looking for people in the maintenance department. Maintenance? I was thinking of the corner office just down from his. I never did visit Personnel and realized I had totally humiliated myself. I left the building feeling a full two feet tall. It was just where God wanted me ... I just didn't know it. I learned that day that there is a big difference between "humility" and "humiliation." Humiliation is what you get when you have not learned to be humble.

> *Likewise you younger people, submit yourselves to your elders. Yes, all of you be submissive to one another, and be clothed with humility, for*
>
> > *"God resists the proud, But gives grace to the humble."*
>
> *Therefore humble yourselves under the mighty hand of God, that He may exalt you in due time.*
>
> 1 PETER 5:5–6

The interesting thing about pride is that you don't have to have anything or be anything to be proud. It is a universal sin, not one exclusive to the rich and powerful. A stubborn resistance to God's grace and forgiveness is one of the worst forms of pride. Mine was rooted in a relentless self-reliance that believed there was nothing I could not do. Well, if there is nothing you can't do, you don't really need God, do you, now? True humility is not walking the planet like some pathetic worm either. It is a profound sense of total dependence on God, knowing that without Him, we are nothing.

The Bible says Moses was the most humble man that ever lived, an interesting handle for a man who faced down the Egyptian Pharaoh, the most powerful man in the world, and led 3.5 million people to freedom. Where did Moses learn such humility? From his abject failure. From his forty years of humiliation, when he ran to the backside of the desert after he tried and failed to liberate his people from the hands of the Egyptians. Moses' failure sowed the seeds for his future success. That is how the principle works.

YOU DON'T HAVE TO HAVE ANYTHING OR BE
ANYTHING TO BE PROUD. IT IS A UNIVERSAL SIN,
NOT ONE EXCLUSIVE TO THE RICH AND POWERFUL.

Continued rejection from the corporate world brought me to a place where I was of some small use to God. On a frightfully cold Winnipeg January day in 1984, I left the house at 8:30 AM, presumably to find a job. At this point, I was looking for any job. En route that morning, I got divinely distracted. I had some friends from church who were attending Bible school and they said I should drop by someday and sit in. Rather than drive past the campus that morning, I turned into the parking lot and took in the morning sessions. As I sat there listening, it wasn't exactly a burning bush experience, but I felt like God said, "This is where you are supposed to be." Imagine Kathy's surprise when she asked me later that day how the job hunting had gone and I told her I had enrolled in Bible school instead. I am not recommending this approach. Women love surprises, but only if they somehow involve diamond earrings or tickets to the ballet.

At any rate, it turned out to be the right thing and I never looked back. God knew that being humbled and humiliated was the very thing that would get me to where I needed to be. I know at about this point some of you are thinking, "Hey, wait a minute, you still don't seem very humble." True humility is not wallowing away in self-loathing. It is, as I said, a total dependency on God, knowing that without Him there is not much we can do. I try to live there every day.

One year, my congregation gave me a plaque that said, "THE WORLD'S MOST HUMBLE PASTOR," but as soon as I put it up on my office wall, they took it away. You get it! But seriously, I learned the hard way where self-reliance gets you. You actually can't *try* to be humble, because if you succeeded and became super-humble you would become proud of being humble and then you would be right back to where you started. Huh? Humility is not an outward appearance but an inward state of the heart.

We cannot be afraid of or despise failure. It is part of life, but maybe more importantly, part of our journey toward our ultimate destiny. It is our failures that will get us there, not our successes. Buried within the pain and failures of life is hidden our greater purpose. So embrace your failures, for they are the key to your success.

Chapter Fifteen

When Life Doesn't Make Sense

If life was fair, Elvis would be alive and all the impersonators would be dead.

— Johnny Carson

IT IS EASY to find stories of how some person—that you don't know and have never met and who lives somewhere else—overcame a horrendous adversity and subsequently went on to change their world and make it a better place. But when we are in the midst of a confusing, painful experience, it is very hard to figure out how to get through the day, let alone see the big picture and a greater purpose.

Sometimes, no matter how good an attitude you manage to maintain, life doesn't make sense and God doesn't seem fair. I don't think it is ever a sin to ask the hard questions of God, as long as you do it with humility and sincerity. If you are not sure about this, go read some of David's psalms.

How long, O Lord? Will You forget me forever?
How long will You hide Your face from me?

PSALM 13:1

Lord, how long will You look on?
Rescue me from their destructions,
My precious life from the lions.

PSALM 35:17

How long, Lord?
Will You be angry forever?
Will Your jealousy burn like fire?

PSALM 79:5

How long, Lord?
Will You hide Yourself forever?
Will Your wrath burn like fire?

PSALM 89:46

Lord, how long will the wicked,
How long will the wicked triumph?

PSALM 94:3

David is far more honest than I would be in prayer. I might think some of these things, but I wouldn't say them out loud (as if it really matters—God knows our thoughts before we think them and words before we speak them, as Psalm 139:4 says, *"For there is not a word on my tongue, But behold, O Lord, You know it altogether"*). I get the distinct impression that David had his fair share of bad days when he felt God was a bit tardy in remedying the situation. The thing to remember is that, in almost every one of these psalms where David is whining, by the end he turns his trust to the Lord and declares God's sovereignty, mercy and loving kindness, as shown in Psalm 13:5–6,

But I have trusted in Your mercy;
My heart shall rejoice in Your salvation.
I will sing to the Lord,
Because He has dealt bountifully with me.

The Bible calls David "a man after God's heart" in Acts 13:22, and yet it is clear he didn't always understand what was going on. There were times when he wasn't sure where God was and life just

194

didn't make sense. If the great King David had these self-doubts, is there any reason to think we can get through life without them? Life is not always going to make sense. Sometimes you will not find the answer this side of heaven, so I am not sure it is worth torturing yourself with it.

As a pastor, I spend a fair bit of time helping people sort through the grief of the death of a loved one. This is usually life's toughest moment. I did a funeral for a man who died of lung cancer at the age of sixty. He had smoked two packs of cigarettes a day for over forty years. His wife sat in my office wailing, "Why, why, why did God take him?" I did not want to be insensitive, so I didn't answer the question, but that one seemed pretty obvious to me. Usually it is not that way, like when a baby dies of a brain tumor, a teen dies in a car accident, a young father dies of a heart attack or a sibling takes their own life. These are painful and unreasonable scenarios.

One of the things that I have learned as a pastor is that, at that moment, "why?" is actually the wrong question. Most of the time, we will not get an answer. Worse yet, like my friend who died of lung cancer, we may get an answer we don't want to hear. I think the better question is "what?" What difference did that person's life make? How are we better people because we knew them? What greater purpose did their life serve? For what grand purpose did God give them to us as a gift, even if their time on earth was too short in our estimation?

I will always remember 2008 as my worst year ever. Or as Homer Simpson reminded Bart when he said he was having his *worst day of his life*, "No Bart, it's your worst day of your life . . . so far . . ."[1] Everything went badly that year. We had all kinds of sickness in our family, I made a very poor financial investment and, worst of all, my older brother Brad broke his neck and then died of cancer. Somehow, by the grace of God, we got through that year. How I managed to stand in the pulpit and encourage the people while I wrestled with my own sense of discouragement is a miracle in itself.

I was always very close to my brother Brad, and even in adult life, he and his family lived only five houses down the street from us. He was a visionary businessman who always saw things long before they were a reality. When he was diagnosed with Stage Four Lymphoma cancer at the age of only fifty-one, we were all thrown aback. He maintained an amazing attitude and endured the brutally aggressive chemotherapy required to attack such an aggressive form of cancer. He lost a lot of weight and all of his hair, and by the end, he looked like an old man. Nevertheless, he endured the treatment and within six months Brad was declared cancer free, and we rejoiced that God had given our family such an immense victory. People generally do not recover from Stage Four cancer. His hair returned, and like Samson, so did his strength. Almost immediately, he was back pursuing life with a flourish.

Brad was an avid skier. He had taught skiing for years at Alberta's Sunshine Village, as well as at several other mountains. As a Level 3 examiner with the Canadian Ski Instructors Alliance, he was one of the instructors that trained other instructors. Shortly after his recovery from cancer, he was out at a local ski area teaching his six-year-old daughter how to ski. In what can only be described as a freak accident, he fell on a beginner run. I rarely ever saw him fall, even on black diamond expert runs, let alone the bunny slope. He had been skiing down the side of the run and slid right into the trees lining the slope. Apparently, his bones were still brittle from the chemo drugs. His right arm was shattered and his neck was broken. He lay on the side of the hill, motionless, paralyzed from the neck down.

The anxiety that followed that day is too painful to even describe, so I will jump forward a few days.

After surgery to bolt his arm back together with metal plates and to insert a complicated titanium apparatus onto his upper vertebrae, Brad was given the diagnosis that he would be a quadriplegic for the rest of his life. His injury was described as a "C3 incomplete." This meant that his spinal column was not entirely damaged and he might recover some feeling or even movement below the neck. They cautioned him about being too optimistic and said that he would never walk again. They also told him he would likely remain in hospital for nine to twelve months as he healed from the acute injury and learned to cope with his disability.

It is really hard to describe the level of heartbreak that comes with a prognosis like this. Aside from the obvious fact that one's life is irrevocably altered, a spinal cord injury has so many other health problems associated with it that your life is essentially consumed by dealing with these other problems. You cannot even control your bladder and bowels, so every four days health workers need to come and disimpact your bowels. I will not even begin to describe it. It is my opinion that a spinal cord injury is possibly the worst thing that could ever happen to you. The upside is that your mind is unaffected and you still think and speak clearly; the downside is that you are trapped in a physical body that will not do what your lucid mind wants it to do.

One day after work, I went down to the rehab hospital for a visit. As Brad lay motionless on his bed, I inappropriately said to him, "So, what are you up to today?"

He responded, "I'm playing tennis." He wasn't being sarcastic; he was mentally engaged in a tennis match. "Yesterday, I went kayaking," he continued. He refused to be a prisoner to a body that had betrayed him and refused to move. He transported himself mentally somewhere every day and imagined everything he would otherwise normally do. As we talked about the summer that was coming up, he insisted that he was going to be out on the lake in his kayak.

"Okay," I said, and not in a tone of disbelief.

Brad was an absolutely stubborn patient. He would not accept his diagnosis and continually told the hospital staff that he was planning on walking out of the hospital the next week. The only thing he did not resist was the physiotherapy, and in fact he insisted on going twice a day instead of only once. After a couple of months of this, they tried to fit him with a motorized wheelchair but he would not cooperate, saying, "What do I need a wheelchair for? I am walking out of here!" Ten weeks after his accident—ten months before they told him he would be released—he walked out of that hospital room. Don't get me wrong, he did not walk well at all. His arms and legs were stiff like boards. At best, he walked like Frankenstein after an all-night bender. Still, it was a remarkable feat. Because of the incomplete nature of his injury, his brain was sending signals to his muscles to fire, often as random and painful spasms. He learned to work with them and his involuntarily stiffened legs were actually capable of carrying his weight.

Once Brad was at home, he continued to make gains. Nevertheless, like anyone, he had his moments of discouragement. During one such period, I had an idea. Steven Fletcher, who was the Member of Parliament for the riding of Charleswood at the time, was a friend of mine. He was the first and only quadriplegic to ever be elected to the House of Commons. He was completely paralyzed from the neck down when the car in which he was travelling struck a moose on the highway. After his recovery, he finished a university degree and was elected to Parliament. He is a true inspiration. I called Steven and asked if he would come and see my brother and encourage him. He readily agreed and his aide brought him over. The first thing out of his mouth when Brad asked him how he could stand being trapped in a wheelchair was, "It sucks." But then he talked about how you need to learn to live beyond the circumstances that you cannot change. These were all things Brad believed and understood, but they are not easy to live out when your body will just not cooperate. I will never forget when Steven asked my brother if he could move any body parts. Brad weakly raised his left arm and moved three fingers.

"Are you kidding me?" Steven replied, "You could fly a plane." It was hard not to laugh.

Five months after the accident, my brother was down at the family cottage. He informed me that this was the day he was going kayaking. "Okay," I said once again, still not in a tone of disbelief. We got him down to the water and helped load him into his kayak. The paddle was going to be a problem, since he did not have the grip to hold onto it. I asked myself, *What would Red Green do in a situation like this?* The answer was clear: duct tape! Fetching a roll of the ubiquitous grey sticky stuff, I duct-taped Brad's hands to the paddle and pushed him out into the lake. He succeeded mostly in just going around in circles, but somehow he managed to make it back to the dock. As awkward and clumsy as he was, we cheered like he had just won an Olympic gold medal. It was no small victory for a man who was told he would never get out of a wheelchair. The thing that he had only dreamed about, laying on his back five months earlier, was now happening in front of our very eyes. If there ever was any doubt, the power of vision punctuated the moment.

The following months were tough, as progress slowed and he seemed to be living in more nerve pain than ever. About a year after the accident, it seemed that things were moving backward. There was something wrong, and unfortunately his doctors did not notice it. The cancer had returned with a vengeance. Eventually he was back in the hospital fighting an old foe, now in a much weakened state.

This time around, the chemotherapy did not work and literally almost killed him. He was in septic shock, comatose and bleeding internally. The intensive care unit was doing what they could and we were just waiting for the news that he was gone.

Then God gave us a little miracle. He woke up from the coma and was perfectly lucid. He started talking about how he was a little disappointed that he was still here. He was completely at peace with his situation. He had no fear, no anxiety and no regrets. Although his body was an absolute mess on the outside, he had a perfect calm on the inside. After a couple of days, he gathered us all around and delivered a short speech: "Everybody is calling me some sort of hero for how I am handling this. I'm not so heroic, I've just run out of options. The only option I have left is to go and be with Jesus. But when you think about it, that is a pretty good option . . . and one a lot of people don't have."

Even in his final days, Brad never lost his positive outlook on life. Realizing his body was going to give way, Brad began to talk joyfully about the next leg of the journey. He started to say things like, "I am ready to go be with Jesus." He also spoke of being reunited with our brother Timothy, who had drowned in front of Brad's four-year-old eyes. A day or two later, he was gone. I thought, *We should be so blessed to face death half as well . . . to be able to leave this world without regret, fear or sorrow.* What my brother found was the joy that comes from within. It has nothing to do with what happens to us on the outside and everything to do with what we know on the inside.

Brad's funeral was the toughest, and yet the easiest, I have ever performed. Hard, because it is never easy to lose a brother, but easy, because he was steadfastly sure of where he was going and it was not "good bye" but "see you later."

There are times when life doesn't make sense. And there are times when it is certainly not fair. It was not fair that my brother had to battle cancer and a spinal cord injury at the same time. It is not fair that Steven Fletcher wakes up every morning unable to move, feed himself or even scratch his nose. Yet, in the midst of his profound disability, he has found his greater purpose. He serves as an MP with passion and irrepressible energy. It is not fair that Stephen Hawking, one of the world's most brilliant minds, has one of the world's most feeble bodies. Suffering from advanced Lou Gehrig's disease (ALS), his twisted little frame is confined to a motorized wheelchair. He is no longer able to speak but has to communicate by means of a computer-generated voice. Yet, he is arguably the preeminent voice in his field of astrophysics. We all carry stories that don't make sense, are not fair and somehow cause us to feel that God is indifferent to our situation. But even though the first two parts may be correct, the last thought is not.

Why do you say, O Jacob,
And speak, O Israel:
"My way is hidden from the Lord,
And my just claim is passed over by my God"?
Have you not known?
Have you not heard?
The everlasting God, the Lord,
The Creator of the ends of the earth,
Neither faints nor is weary.
His understanding is unsearchable.
He gives power to the weak,
And to those who have no might He increases strength.
Even the youths shall faint and be weary,
And the young men shall utterly fall,
But those who wait on the Lord
Shall renew their strength;
They shall mount up with wings like eagles,
They shall run and not be weary,

They shall walk and not faint.

ISAIAH 40:27–31

Life is not fair, but God is. Isaiah reminds us not to think that our "just claim" has been passed over. God's understanding is unsearchable. We can never fully understand what He is up to. We only get a glimpse. Whatever situation we find ourselves in, we must take a big dose of the sovereignty of God and say, "I don't get it, but I need to trust that God knows what He is doing."

When our kids were younger, they had an expression that children everywhere use. If one sibling got something and the others did not, they would immediately object, "Hey that's not fair."

I would respond, "You're right; it's not fair. Get used to it—life is not fair!" I know that sounds like a hard-nosed parent, but it is one of the most important lessons we can learn, and the sooner we learn it, the better. How is it that children come into this world with such a well-developed sense of entitlement? It is part of our sinful nature. Eve couldn't stand it that, even though she lived in paradise, there might be something else she was missing out on. She ate the forbidden fruit and gave it to her husband Adam too. She was the first woman in history to eat her family out of house and home.

IF GOD GAVE US ALL WHAT WE DESERVE, HE WOULD HAVE TO SEND EACH ONE OF US DIRECTLY TO HELL. TRUST ME, YOU DO NOT WANT WHAT YOU DESERVE.

This attitude of entitlement will follow us our entire lives if we don't deal with it and begin to live with a sense of profound gratitude, knowing that we don't actually deserve any good thing. If God gave us all what we deserve, He would have to send each one of us directly to hell; do not pass Go, do not collect $200. Trust me on this one, you do not want what you deserve and you do not want your "just claim"!

It's not fair that I was born in the first world and not the third world. It is not fair that I grew up in a home where there was food on the table for every single mealtime. It is not fair that in the morning I had to decide which pair of shoes I was going to wear to school because I had more than one. It is not fair that I got a free education courtesy of the Canadian taxpayer. It is not fair that when I got sick my parents could take me to a doctor and we never even got sent a bill. It is not fair that we could go to church every Sunday and worship God without fear of being arrested or persecuted. It is not fair that I could walk down the streets of our neighbourhood after dark without worry of being mugged or robbed. It is not fair that I grew up in a home with a live-in maid and I didn't even have to make my own bed in the morning. It is not fair that we had cars in the driveway and I was never once responsible to fill up the gas tank. (If it was empty, I just took the other car.) It is not fair that when I die I will go to heaven to live with Jesus in paradise, forever. There is no question about it . . . life is not fair.

What can we do when life doesn't make sense? Nothing! There is nothing we can do about it, so we had better learn to accept the good and the bad and thank God for the good.

> *God, give me grace to accept with serenity*
> *the things that cannot be changed,*
> *Courage to change the things*
> *which should be changed,*
> *and the Wisdom to distinguish*
> *the one from the other.*
> *Living one day at a time,*
> *Enjoying one moment at a time,*

Accepting hardship as a pathway to peace,
Taking, as Jesus did,
This sinful world as it is,
Not as I would have it,
Trusting that You will make all things right,
If I surrender to Your will,
So that I may be reasonably happy in this life,
And supremely happy with You forever in the next.
Amen.

— Reinhold Niebuhr[2]

Chapter Sixteen

Conclusion

I expect to pass through this world but once; any good thing therefore that I can do, or any kindness that I can show to any fellow creature, let me do it now; let me not defer or neglect it, for I shall not pass this way again.

— Stephen Grellet[1]

HERE IS WHAT we need to know about purpose: purpose is not so much about what we do, but who we are. The "who we are" endures long past the "what we do."

The heroes of the past are remembered more for who they were than for what they did. Although I have told many of their stories, few of us could list the specifics of what they did. We remember their heart, passion and burning zeal to make the world a better place. The Albert Schweitzers, Alfred Nobels, Martin Luther Kings and Mother Teresas did what they did because of who they were.

It is no different in our own lives. What we do in life has very little power to carry vision and propel us forward into our own grand purpose. The details become boring and tedious without an underlining greater purpose born out of our character, vision and passion. Our world desperately needs each one of us to discover why we are here. None of us wants to go through life merely consuming oxygen and not making a contribution to the overall good. It is not easy, but it is not complicated either.

205

Life is hard, life isn't fair and sometimes life doesn't make sense, but God in His omniscience has placed us in the midst of it all to discover our greater purpose. He has gone to great lengths to select you from trillions of possible permutations of sperm and egg, made you to be part of an arguably dysfunctional family, thrust you into a community of wonderfully quirky people, surrounded you with seven billion other diverse humans who have all been placed on a uniquely constructed planet that is most likely the only place that could even sustain life in an unimaginable universe which spans 13.67 billion light years. There can be no way that any of that is by mere chance or coincidence, and there has got to be a specific divine purpose for your existence in this moment of time and space. God has already laid out the grand plan for your life; you just have to figure out what it is and start doing it. You have the easy part, because chances are, it is right in front of your face.

We start to see it when we metaphorically (and often literally) lift up our eyes. The key is not to wait for a lightning bolt from heaven, but rather, to simply serve where we have opportunity, and usually right where we are. We begin by realigning our passions with God's passions, reassigning our gifting to Him and rediscovering the joy of serving others. If we will do our part, God will do His part and direct our path—it is a promise. Proverbs 16:9 says, *"A man's heart plans his way, but the Lord directs his steps."*

We really only have one job, and that is to find our place in God's great big space. Now put down this book and get started!

Acknowledgements

No one ever writes a book alone. It is almost always a collective effort of people contributing stories, ideas and perspectives, which results in a vastly superior final product. There are far too many people to mention, but there are a few who have made an invaluable contribution.

Special thanks needs to go to: my wife, Kathy, who endured months of the writing process and the painful rereading of the rewrites so that I could get her coveted feedback; to Chris Wahl, for producing an outstanding book cover that almost tells the story alone; to Marcia Hamm, for the many hours producing an initial edit of the first draft; and to editor Larissa Bartos, who journeyed alongside all of us to produce a professionally edited and formatted final copy. THANK YOU.

NOTES

CHAPTER ONE

[1] Terry Goodkind, *Confessor* (New York: Tor Books, 2007), 756.

[2] M. J. Simpson, *Hitchhiker: A Biography of Douglas Adams*, first US ed. (Boston: Justin Charles & Co., 2003), 340.

[3] Douglas Adams and Eoin Colfer, *A Hitchhiker's Guide to the Galaxy* (London: Pan Am Books, 1979).

[4] Ibid., 110.

[5] Stephen Hawking, *A Brief History of Time* (Toronto: Bantam Books, 1988), 174–175.

[6] *Curiosity: Did God Create the Universe?* Season 1, Episode 1, first broadcast Aug. 7, 2011, by Discovery Channel. Series created by Tom Leach. Produced by Darlow Smithson Productions (as Darlow Smithson Productions Ltd.) for Discovery Channel. Accessed online as "There is no God. There is no Fate." YouTube video, 1:33. Posted by "stepore," August 15, 2011, https://youtu.be/7L7VTdzuY7Y.

[7] Goodkind, *Confessor*, 756.

[8] Hugh Ross, Kenneth Samples and Mark Clark, "Appendix B: Probabilities for Life on Earth," in *Lights in the Sky and Little Green Men: A Rational Christian Look at UFOs and Extraterrestrials* (Colorado Springs, CO: NavPress, 2002).

[9] Hugh Ross, "Astronomical Evidences for a Personal, Transcendent God," in J. P. Moreland (ed.), *The Creation Hypothesis* (Downers Grove: IVP, 1994), 170.

[10] Joseph S. Exell, ed., *The Biblical Illustrator* (Electronic Database Copyright © 2002, 2003, 2006, 2011 by Biblesoft, Inc.) accessed June 13, 2015, http://biblehub.com/sermons/pub/faith_in_prayer.htm, s.v. "Matthew 21:22."

[11] Francis Collins, *The Language of God: A Scientist Presents Evidence for Belief* (New York: Free Press/Simon & Shuster, 2006).

[12] Collins, *Language of God*, 140.

CHAPTER TWO

[1] Walter Mischel, *The Marshmallow Test: Mastering Self-Control* (Boston: Little, Brown and Company, 2014).

[2] *The Simpsons: Treehouse of Horror IV*, season 5 episode 5, broadcast on October 28, 1993 by Fox Broadcasting Company. Directed by David Silverman and co-written by Conan O'Brien, Bill Oakley, Josh Weinstein, Greg Daniels, Dan McGrath, and Bill Canterbury.

[3] Ibid.

[4] Steve May, *The Story File: 1,001 Contemporary Illustrations for Speakers, Writers and Preachers* (Peabody, MA :Hendrickson Publishers, 2000), 7.

[5] Victor Frankl, *Man's Search for Meaning* (Boston: Beacon Press, 2006), 56–57.

CHAPTER THREE

[1] Jay Yarow, "Bill Gates Has Given Away $28 Billion Since 2007, Saving 6 Million Lives," January 14, 2012, http://www.businessinsider.com/bill-gates-infographic-2012-1.

[2] Oliver Harvey, "I'm not leaving the money to my kids... it wouldn't be good for them or society," *The Sun*, September 21, 2010, http://www.thesun.co.uk/sol/homepage/features/3144438/Bill-Gates-Im-not-leaving-my-fortune-to-my-children.html

[3] Bob Buford, *Finishing Well: What People Who Really Live Do Differently* (Brentwood, TN: Integrity Publishers/Thomas Nelson, 2004), 25.

CHAPTER FOUR

[1] "Office of the United Nations High Commissioner for Refugees - Nobel Lecture: Refugee Problems and Their Solutions," Nobelprize.org, Nobel Media AB 2014, June 13, 2015, http://www.nobelprize.org/nobel_prizes/peace/laureates/1954/refugees-lecture.html#not.

[2] Frederic Golden, "The Worst And The Brightest: For a century, the Nobel Prizes have recognized achievement—the good, the bad and the crazy," *Time*, October 16, 2000, http://content.time.com/time/magazine/article/0,9171,998209,00.html

[3] Goodkind, *Confessor*, 756.

[4] Steven R. Covey, *7 Habits of Highly Effective People* (Old Tappan, NJ: Free Press, 1989), 95.

CHAPTER FIVE

1 Slash (performed by Slash and Mark Lanegan), "So Long Sin City," song from the movie soundtrack *This is Not a Movie*, written and directed by Olallo Rubio, 2011 (Mexico).

2 Joel Osteen, "Interview With Joel Osteen," Interviewed by Larry King, *CNN Larry King Live*, Aired June 20, 2005. Online transcript found at http://www.cnn.com/TRANSCRIPTS/0506/20/lkl.01.html.

3 Rachel Held Evans, "Why millennials are leaving the church," *CNN Belief Blog*, July 27, 2013, http://religion.blogs.cnn.com/2013/07/27/why-millennials-are-leaving-the-church/.

CHAPTER SIX

1 *Back to the Future*, Universal Pictures, July 3, 1985, written by Robert Zemeckis and Bob Gale, directed by Robert Zemeckis, produced by Bob Gale and Neil Canton.

2 Dayna Dunteman, "Roger Crawford," *Sacramento (sacmag.com)*, July 2014, posted October 26, http://www.sacmag.com/Sacramento-Magazine/July-2004/Personality-Roger-Crawford. Also ref. Roger Crawford, *Playing Heart From the Heart: A Portrait in Courage* (New York: Crown Publishing Group, 1998).

3 Jack Canfield, Mark Victor Hansen, and Amy Newmark, *Chicken Soup for the Soul 20th Anniversary Edition* (Cos Cob, CT: Chicken Soup for the Soul Publishing, 2013), 291.

4 Ibid., 292.

5 Ibid.

6 Ibid., 293.

CHAPTER SEVEN

1 Jarod Kintz, *This Book Has No Title*, Amazon Digital Services, Inc., March 22, 2012.

2 US Center for Disease Control and Prevention, "Increasing Prevalence of Parent-Reported Attention-Deficit/Hyperactivity Disorder Among Children --- United States, 2003 and 2007," November 12, 2010, http://www.cdc.gov/mmwr/preview/mmwrhtml/mm5944a3.htm.

[3] Smith Corona Corporation, "History of Smith Corona," online multimedia presentation, http://www.smithcorona.com/history.

[4] IBM, "1995," https://www-03.ibm.com/ibm/history/history /year_1995.html.

CHAPTER EIGHT

[1] Leon McBeth, *The First Baptist Church of Dallas: Centennial History (1868–1968)* (Grand Rapids, MI: Zondervan, 1968), 240–347.

[2] Charles Paul Conn, *Making It Happen* (New York: Berkley, 1983), 95.

CHAPTER NINE

[1] Lou Holtz, *Winning Every Day: The Game Plan for Success*, first ed. (New York: Harper Business, 1998), 121.

[2] Not sourced. Most often attributed to Vincent Thomas Vince Lombardi, former football coach of the Green Bay Packers 1959–1968.

[3] Quote attributed to Martina Navratilova. See Barry Popik, "Entry from September 22, 2012," http://www.barrypopik.com/index.php /new_york_city/entry/whoever_said_its_not_whether_you_win_or_los e_that_counts_probably_lost.

[4] The New York Times Company, "WASHINGTON TALK: BRIEFING; Pryor 'Born Yesterday'," March 27, 1987, http://www.nytimes.com/1987/03/27/us/washington-talk-briefing-pryor-born-yesterday.html.

[5] Bruce Feldman, "Top 10 blunders in history," *Bruce Feldman Blog*, May 30, 2007, http://insider.espn.go.com/ncf/blog?name=feldman_bruce &id=2887178.

[6] Variant of original quote: "If you don't know where you're going, you might not get there." Yogi Berra, *When You Come to a Fork in the Road, Take It!: Inspiration and Wisdom from One of Baseball's Greatest Heroes* (New York: Hyperion, 2002), 53.

[7] *The Bucket List*, Castle Rock Entertainment, December 15, 2007, Directed by Rob Reiner.

[8] CBC/Radio-Canada, "Into the Death Zone" *The Fifth Estate*, Season 38, Broadcast September 12, 2012. http://www.cbc.ca/fifth/episodes /2012-2013/into-the-death-zone.

[9] CBC/Radio-Canada, "Calgary man says Everest rescue was 'the only thing to do'," *CBC News Calgary*, June 02, 2006, http://www.cbc.ca

/news/canada/calgary/calgary-man-says-everest-rescue-was-the-only-thing-to-do-1.578945.

CHAPTER TEN

[1] *Batman Begins*, released June 15, 2005 by Warner Bros. Pictures, http://www.imdb.com/title/tt0372784/quotes.

[2] *The Truman Show*, released June 5, 1998, Paramount Pictures, http://www.imdb.com/title/tt0120382/quotes.

[3] Erika J. Waters, "Modern MARCO: From the Mackle Brothers to today," http://themihs.com/historical-photos/modern-mar/.

CHAPTER ELEVEN

[1] Rick Warren, *The Purpose Driven Life* (Grand Rapids, MI: Zondervan, 1997).

[2] A. Larry Ross Communications, "Rick Warren's 'The Purpose Driven Life' Celebrates 10 Years," *CharismaNews*, October 21, 2012, http://www.charismanews.com/us/34357-rick-warrens-the-purpose-driven-life-celebrates-10-years.

[3] http://www.goodreads.com/quotes/1154643-the-problem-with-the-world-is-that-we-draw-the. (Mother Teresa quotes are difficult to source as she did not do any writing herself. It is even possible she did not even say some of the things attributed to her.)

[4] Philip Yancey, *Where Is God When It Hurts?* (Grand Rapids, MI: Zondervan, 2009), 57.

[5] Tony Campolo, "Find Your Own Calcutta," July 6, 2011, http://www.redletterchristians.org/find-your-own-calcutta/.

[6] Rachel E. Rigdon and Thomas G. Webster, "His Mother's Child: On Susanna Wesley's Great Influence Upon Her Son, John Wesley," in partial fulfillment of the course requirements for Dr. Tamara Lewis' United Methodist History course at Perkins School of Theology, Southern Methodist University, Fall 2013.

[7] *Moberly Monitor-Index* (March 6, 1970), 3.

[8] William Wright, *All the Pain Money Can Buy: The Life of Christina Onassis* (New York: Simon & Schuster, 2000), 200.

[9] *The Jerk*, Universal Pictures, December 14, 1979. Directed by Carl Reiner. Written by Steve Martin, Carl Gottlieb, and Michael Elias.

[10] Source unknown.

CHAPTER TWELVE

[1] Albert Schweitzer, Antje Bultmann Lemke, Trans., *Out of My Life and Thought: An Autobiography*, 60th edition (Baltimore, MD: JHU Press, 2009).

James Brabazon, *Albert Schweitzer: A Biography*, 2nd edition (Syracuse, NY: Syracuse University Press, 2000).

George N. Marshal and David Poling, *Schweitzer: A Biography* (Baltimore, MD: JHU Press, 1971).

[2] Albert Schweitzer, *Quest of the Historical Jesus*, first English edition, Trans. William Montgomery (London: A. & C. Black, Ltd, 1910). Accessible online at http://www.earlychristianwritings.com/schweitzer/

[3] P. K. Hallinan, *A Life That Matters: Five Steps to Making a Difference* (Grand Rapids, MI: Kregel, 2012), 133.

[4] Father Brian Kolodiejchuk, Ed., *Mother Teresa: Come Be My Light* (New York: Doubleday, 2007), 34.

CHAPTER THIRTEEN

[1] Doug Larson, columnist for *Green Bay Press-Gazette,* exact reference unknown.

[2] Dr. A. N. P. Ummerkutty, *Great Sayings & Quotations* (Tamilnadu, India: Sura Books, 2014), 68.

[3] Marion Mill Preminger, *All I Want is Everything* (New York: Funk and Wagnalls, 1957), 279.

[4] Aleksandr Solzhenitsyn, Thomas P. Whitney, Trans., *The Gulag Archepelago 1918–1956: An Experiment in Literary Investigation* (New York: Harper & Row, 1974).

CHAPTER FOURTEEN

[1] Olga Kharif and Roger O. Crockett, "Motorola's Market Share Mess," *Bloomberg Business*, July 10, 2008, http://www.bloomberg.com/bw /stories/2008-07-10/motorolas-market-share-messbusinessweek-business-news-stock-market-and-financial-advice. See also, Associated Press, "Motorola Suspends Dividend Amid $3.6 Billion Loss," *New York Times*, February 3, 2009, http://www.nytimes.com/2009/02/04 /business/04motorola.html?_r=0.

² Oliver Moore, "Maritime community hits jackpot, with lottery winners in their midst," *Globe and Mail*, published Thursday, November 4, 2010, updated August 23, 2012, http://www.theglobeandmail.com/news/national/maritime-community-hits-jackpot-with-lottery-winners-in-their-midst/article4262816/

³ Paul W. Brand and Philip Yancey, *Pain: The Gift Nobody Wants* (New York: HarperCollins Publishers, 1993).

⁴ Francis Rolt-Wheeler, *Thomas Alva Edison* (New York: The Macmillan Company, 1915), 177.

⁵ City of Enterprise, "History of Enterprise," http://www.enterpriseal.gov/#!history-of-enterprise/c6gw.

⁶ Sun-Maid, "History of Raisins and Dried Fruit," http://www.sunmaid.com/history-of-raisins-and-dried-fruit.html

⁷ The Canadian Press, "Rick Hansen's anniversary relay ends in Vancouver," *CTV News Vancouver*, May 22, 2010, http://bc.ctvnews.ca/rick-hansen-s-anniversary-relay-ends-in-vancouver-1.830361

CHAPTER FIFTEEN

¹ *The Simpsons Movie*, released July 21, 2007, by 20ᵗʰ Century Fox. Directed by David Silverman.

² Fred R. Shapiro, "Who Wrote the Serenity Prayer?" *The Chronicle for Higher Education*, April 28, 2014, http://chronicle.com/article/Who-Wrote-the-Serenity-Prayer-/146159/

CHAPTER SIXTEEN

¹ (Sometimes attributed to Stephen Grellet). Susan Ratcliffe, ed., *Oxford Treasury of Sayings and Quotations*, Fourth Edition (Oxford: Oxford University Press, 2011), 482.